大展好書　好書大展
品嘗好書　冠群可期

大展好書　好書大展

品嘗好書・　冠群可期

中英文對照武學(4)

李壽堂 編著　　張連友 校訂

32式

太極劍

學與練

附VCD

大展出版社有限公司

32式太極劍學與練
Study and Practice of 32-form Tai Chi Sword

作者　李壽堂

Writer　　Shoutang　Li

翻譯者　北美意源書社

姜淑霞　崔　婧

Translator　　Shuxia Jiang, Yiyuan Martial Arts Books. North America

Jing Cui, Yiyuan Martial Arts Books, North America

作者李壽堂和張連友的練功照

張潤梅演示的32式太極劍

前　言

　　太極劍是屬於太極拳系統的一種劍術套路，它兼有太極拳和劍術的特點，具有與太極拳相同的健身價值。本書介紹的這套32式太極劍是20世紀60年代初由國家體委組織老一輩太極拳名家在傳統楊氏太極劍套路基礎上改編的。全部動作除「起式」和「收式」之外，共選定了32個主要姿勢動作。整個套路分爲四組，每組八個動作，從起式到收式往返兩個來回，練習時間需要三分鐘左右。動作中包括（抽、帶、撩、刺、擊、掛、點、劈、截、托、掃、攔、抹等）13種主要劍法和各種身法、步法。既可單人獨練，又可集體練習。

　　透過這些主要姿勢動作的練習，一可強身健體，二可爲練習難度較大的劍術套路打下基礎，同時，可以表演，增強練習者的鍛鍊興趣。32式太極劍是全民健身運動中的一項很好的健身運動項目，是中國武術段位制「四段」太極劍考評技術。

Preface

Tai Chi sword is born from Tai Chi Chuan. It has the features of both Tai Chi and sword skills, and provides the same health benefits of both. Based on Yang style Tai Chi, the 32–form Tai Chi Sword introduced in this book was created at the beginning of the 60's by experienced masters, who were organized by Chinese Sports Committee. Excluding the opening and closing movements, the entire set includes 32 movements, which are divided into four groups of eight. To finish the routine, from the Opening to the Closing, go back and forth twice. In this form, there are 13 types of sword techniques and slide sideward, and various body movements and steps. It can be practiced individually or in a group. Going through these main postures and movements does not only promote one's health, but it can also be used in performance. At the same time it forms a foundation for further practice of more difficult sword forms. 32– form Tai Chi Sword is a valuable sport for improving one's health. It's also certified as a Level Four technique by the Chinese Wushu Certification System.

目　錄

Content

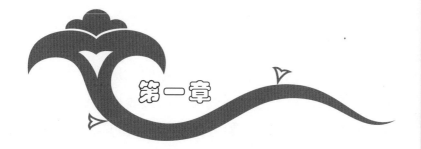

第一章

劍的結構、各部名稱及規格

Chapter 1　Structure, Component Names, and Standard of the Swords

劍是中國很古老的一種兵器，被譽為「百兵之君」。

The sword is an ancient weapon in China, given the name "the king of weapons".

劍在中國出現很早，至今有三千多年的歷史。劍的外形構造及製造材料隨時代的發展不斷地變化。其外形由劍身、劍柄兩大部分組成，劍身為雙刃，有劍尖、劍鋒、劍脊，劍柄有護手、劍柄、劍首。古代劍較短，形如匕首，隨時代的發展由短變長，到戰國後期普遍為1公尺以上；製造材料隨時代的發展經歷了由青銅、鐵到鋼的過程。

The sword has been used in China for approximately three thousand years. Its appearance, structure and material have been continually changing. A sword consists of two parts: a sword blade which includes a tip, double edges and a spine; a hilt that includes a guard, a grip and a pommel. An ancient sword was much shorter and resembled a dagger. Over the years, it became longer and longer. By the end of the Warring States Period, it was more than a meter long. Developed over the ages, the material used for sword also experienced changes from bronze to iron to steel.

劍作為一種古老的兵器，曾在古代戰爭中發揮了重要的主導作用，但隨著時代的發展，兵器種類的增多，其在軍事上的作用相對有所下降。劍作為權貴身份的象徵，文人、雅士、達官貴人均配掛劍器，其劍術與舞蹈相結合成為一種娛樂表演、觀賞的項目。到現代，劍及其劍術已附屬於各拳種、各門派器械，失其早年的主體地位。當今的擊劍、舞劍，成為習武思奮、健身、表演、抒情的全民健身的重要運動項目。

As a weapon, the sword had always played a major role in warfare. However, with constant development of new weapons, the sword's functions as a military weapon gradually weakened as time passed, and instead was worn by scholars, gentlemen, bureaucrats, and aristocrats as a decoration and a symbol of social status. Swordplay, combined with dance, became a performance for entertainment and appreciation. The sword had lost its early eminent position as a weapon and has become an equipment of Wushu sports. Nowadays, swordplay has become a sport for performance, the improvement of health, and the building of characters.

太極劍是近百年來在太極拳的基礎上產生的，其風格特點與太極拳一脈相承。現將當今普遍使用的太極劍結構各部名稱及一般規格要求介紹如下。

Based on Tai Chi Chuan, Tai Chi sword has developed for

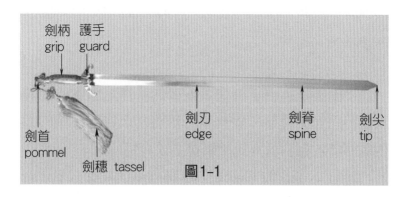

hundreds of years and inherited all the features of Tai Chi. The following are the standard and component's names of the sword that are generally used today.

一、劍的結構和各部名稱（圖1-1）

1. The structure and components of the sword (Figure 1-1)

二、當今常用太極劍在武術比賽中的規格

1. 劍的長度

以直臂垂肘反手持劍的姿勢為準，劍尖不得低於本人的耳上端。

2. The standards of Tai Chi sword used for competition

（1）Size

Let the arm hang down and hold the sword pointing up. The

劍柄 grip
護手 guard
劍首 pommel
劍穗 tassel
劍刃 edge
劍脊 spine
劍尖 tip

圖1-1

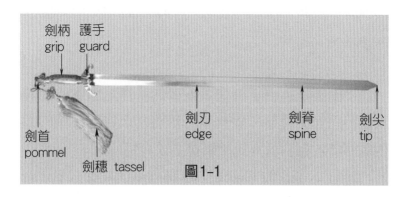

14

32 式太極劍 學與練

tip of the sword should not be lower than the upper edge of the ear.

2. 劍的重量

包括劍穗，供成人男子使用的劍不得輕於0.6公斤，供成年女子使用的劍不得輕於0.5公斤，供少年兒童使用的劍不限重量。

(2) Weight

Including the tassel, the sword for an adult man should not be lighter than 0.6 kg and 0.5kg for an adult woman. There is no restriction for children.

3. 劍身的硬度

劍垂直倒置，劍尖觸地，劍身不得彎曲；或以劍尖至劍柄20公分處為測量點，測量點距地面的垂直距離不得少於10公分（圖1-2）。

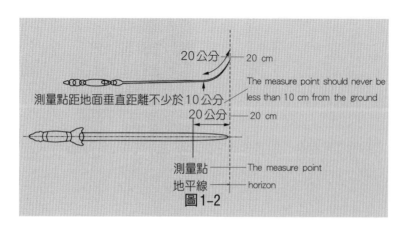

圖1-2

(3) Hardness

Hold the sword with the tip pointing downward and touch-ing the ground. The sword should be able to support itself with-out bending. The other way to measure it is at about 20cm from the tip. The measure point should never be less than 10cm from the ground (Figure 1-2).

4. 劍穗

長短、顏色無限制。

(4) Tassel

There is no demand for the color and size.

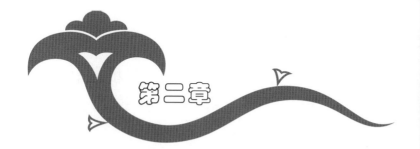

第二章

32式太極劍的基本技術

Chapter 2 Basic Technique of 32-form Tai Chi Sword

第一節 手型與手法

Section 1 Hand Forms and Hand Movements

一、手 型

太極劍的手型主要是劍指，即中指和食指伸直併攏，其餘三指屈於手心，拇指壓在無名指和小指第一指節上（圖2-1）。

【要領】

中指與食指要併攏伸直，不要分開。

1. Hand Forms

The main hand form is the Sword Fingers(Jian zhi). To form the Sword Fingers, extend the index finger and middle finger together and bend the other two fingers to the palm with the thumb pressing on their first knuckle(Figure 2–1).

Key Points

The middle finger and the index finger should be close to each other. They cannot be apart.

二、手 法

太極劍的手法包括持劍和握劍兩種方法。

1. 持 劍

手心緊貼護手，食指附於劍柄，拇指和其餘三指扣緊護手兩側，劍脊輕貼於小臂後側（圖2-2a、圖2-2b）。

【要領】

手應緊握劍，使劍身與地面基本垂直，注意劍刃不要觸及身體。

2. Hand Movements

Hand Movement in Tai Chi Sword means the ways of holding a sword. There are two ways: carrying and gripping.

(1) Carrying

The palm presses around the hand guard of the sword tightly

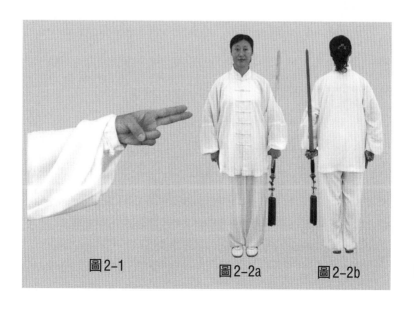

圖2-1　　　　圖2-2a　　　　圖2-2b

with the index finger resting on the handle, the thumb and other three fingers supporting sides of the hand guard. The spine of the sword contacts with the backside of the arm (Figure 2–2a, Figure 2–2b).

Key Points

The hand should hold the sword tightly, keeping the sword blade perpendicular to the ground. Do not touch one's body with the edges of the sword.

2. 握 劍

握劍主要是指右手靈活運使劍的方法。右手握劍主要有以下幾種具體方法。

(2) Gripping

The sword gripping here refers to the methods for the right hand to use a sword flexibly during the movements. Several methods are described here.

(1)螺把握劍

手握劍柄，虎口對準劍上刃，食指、中指、無名指和小指第一指節緊扣劍柄，依次成「螺旋」型，拇指緊扣於食指第一指節上，以食指第二指節緊靠護手（劍格），腕關節微下屈（圖2-3）。

a. Gripping Spirally

Grip the handle of the sword with "tiger mouth" (the part between the thumb and the first finger) against the hand guard, aligned with the edge of the blade. Grasp the handle with four fingers and bend the thumb to press tightly on the first knuckle of the index finger. The second knuckle of the index finger is close to the hand guard. Bend the wrist down slightly (Figure 2–3).

(2)滿把握劍

虎口正對護手（劍格），五指如同平握拳環握劍柄，拇指屈壓於食指第三指節上，腕部挺直（圖2-4）。

b. Fully Gripping

With the "tiger mouth" (the part between the thumb and

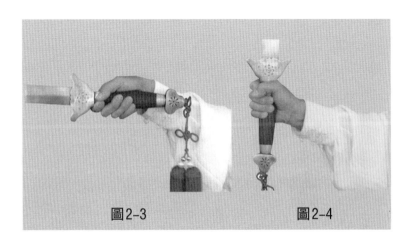

圖2-3　　　　圖2-4

21

the first finger）against the hand guard, the four fingers grip the handle. The thumb bends, pressing on the third knuckle of the index finger. The wrist is stretched（Figure 2–4）.

（3）鉗把握劍

虎口靠近護手（劍格），以食指、拇指和虎口的夾持之勁將劍柄鉗住，其餘三指自然附於劍柄（圖2-5）。

c. Clamping the Sword

With "tiger mouth" close to the hand guard, the index finger and the thumb clamp the handle while the other three fingers attaching to the handle naturally（Figure 2–5）.

（4）墊把握劍

其方法與螺把握劍基本相同，只是拇指伸直，緊

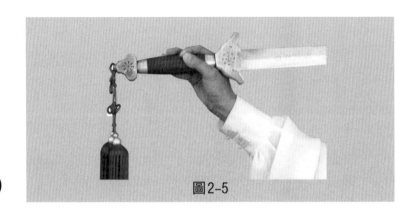

圖2-5

扣於劍柄，食指伸直附於護手上，其餘三指屈握劍柄（圖2-6）。

d. Underlying Gripping

Similar to "Gripping Spirally", Put the thumb against the handle and the index finger on the hand guard. The other three fingers bend and grasp the handle (Figure 2-6).

【要領】

握劍時要掌握手腕鬆、手指活、手心空的三要領。握劍以拇指、中指和無名指為主，食指、小指配合，隨動作的變化時鬆時緊，自然順遂，不可僵握。

Key Points

When gripping the sword, keep the wrist relaxed, the fingers flexible and the palm empty (a bit away from the handle). The force of the grip comes mainly from the thumb, the middle finger

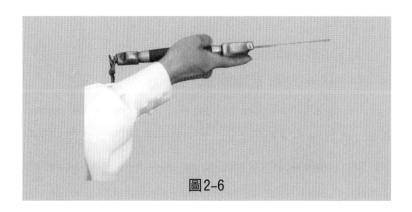

圖2-6

and the third finger, with the index finger and little finger co-operating. Connect the motions naturally; do not be rigid.

第二節　步型與步法

Section 2　Foot Positions and Foot Movements

一、步　型

1. 弓　步

前腳尖向前，全腳著地，屈膝半蹲，大腿接近水平，膝部約與腳尖垂直；另一腿自然伸直，腳尖裏扣斜向前，全腳著地，兩腳橫向距離10～20公分（圖2-7）。

【要領】

前腿屈膝不可超過腳尖，後腿不要僵挺，兩腳不可踩在一條直線上，更不能左右交叉。

1. Foot Positions

(1) Bow Step (Gong Bu)

One foot takes a step forward and is placed on the ground. Bend the knee in a half squat, the thigh parallel to the ground; the knee should be never beyond the toes. The other leg straightens naturally, the toes pointing about 45° inwards and the entire foot placed on the ground. The feet stand on two parallel lines separately, which are about 10 to 20 cm apart (Figure 2–7).

Key Points

The front knee should not go beyond the toes. The other leg should not be rigid. The feet should not be aligned line or on intersecting lines.

2. 虛 步

後腳斜向前45°，屈膝下蹲，全腳著地；另一腿微屈，前腳掌或腳跟虛著地（圖2-8）。

【要領】

支撐腳全腳著地，承擔全身重量的80%，另一腿膝部要微屈，不可挺直，承擔全身重量的20%。

圖2-7

圖2-8

(2) Empty Step（Xu Bu）

Bend one knee with the entire foot placed on the ground and toes outward 45°. Bend the other knee slightly with either only the forefoot or only the heel of the foot on the ground（Figure 2-8）.

Key Points

The supporting foot touches the ground fully upholding 80% of the weight, and the other leg bends slightly, taking 20% of the weight.

3. 丁步

一腿屈膝半蹲，全腳著地；另一腿屈膝，以前腳掌或腳尖點於支撐腿腳內側（圖2-9）。

【要領】

兩腳間的距離不可超過一腳，虛實分明。

(3) T-shape Step（Ding Bu）

Bend one leg in half squat with the foot placed on the ground. Bend the other knee with its forefoot or toes touching the ground at the inside of the supporting foot（Figure 2-9）.

Key Points

The distance between the feet should not be over a foot（12 inches）. The two legs each support a different amount of weight.

4. 獨立步

一腿自然直立，支撐體重站穩；另一腿在體前或體側屈膝提起，高與腰齊，小腿自然下垂，腳面平展，腳尖自然向下（圖2-10）。

【要領】

支撐腿自然直立，支撐腳要似吸盤緊貼地面，另一腳提起，腳尖不可向上蹺。

(4) One Leg Stand or Independent Step (Du Li Bu)

One leg stands straight naturally, supporting the weight. The other one lifted with the knee bent in front or at side of the body at waist level. The foot should be stretched and the toes pointing downward naturally (Figure 2-10).

Key Points

The supporting leg stands naturally straight and the support-

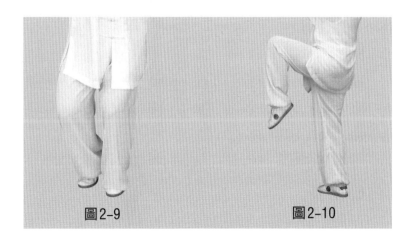

圖2-9   圖2-10

ing foot on the ground like a suction cup. Lift the other leg, but do not raise the toes.

5. 歇 步

兩腿屈膝全蹲，前腳尖外展，全腳著地；後腳尖向前，膝部附於前腿外側，腳跟離地，臀部接近腳跟（圖2-11）。

【要領】

前腳腳跟不得離地，兩腳距離要恰當，不可過大，後腿與前腳不相接觸，形成跪腿。

(5) Low Squat with Crossed legs (Xie Bu)

Bend the two legs in a squat. The front toes turns outward with the sole fully touching the ground. The knee behind attaches to the inside of the front knee with the toes pointing forward and the heel is lifted off the ground. The buttocks should be close to the heel as if sitting on it (Figure 2–11).

Key Points

Do not lift the front heel off the ground. The distance between the feet should be appropriate. The leg behind should not touch the front foot or kneel down.

6. 仆 步

一腿屈膝全蹲，膝與腳尖稍外展；另一腿自然伸直，平鋪接近地面，腳尖內扣，兩腳全腳著地，不可掀起（圖2-12）。

【要領】

屈膝全蹲，膝部要與腳尖方向一致，不得裏扣；平鋪伸直一腿腳尖應裏扣，與腿部成90°。

(6) Crouch Stance or Crouch Step（Pu Bu）

One leg bends in a squat, the knee and toes pointing slightly outwards. Extend the other leg close to the ground, toes pointing inward. Both feet are fully placed on the ground（Figure 2-12）.

Key Points

Bend the knee in a full squat and point the knee in the same direction as the toes; do not turn it inward. The toes of the ex-

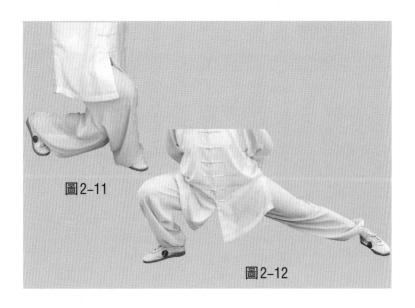

圖2-11

圖2-12

tended leg should turn inward to form an angle of 90° with the squatting leg.

7. 側弓步

此步型介於弓步與仆步之間，一腿屈膝下蹲，另一腿向體側伸出成高仆步狀（圖2-13）。

【要領】

支撐重心一腳，膝部不可超過腳尖，兩腳接近平行。

(7) Side Bow Stance or Step（Ce Gong Bu）

This stance is similar to both the Bow Stance and Crouch Stance. One leg bends in squat and the other leg naturally extends sideward as if in a high Crouch Stance（Figure 2–13）.

Key Points

The knee of the supporting leg should not go beyond the

圖2-13

toes. The two feet are paralleled.

二、步 法

1. 上 步
後腳向前上一步。

2. 活 步
前腳隨動作稍移動。

3. 退 步
前腳後退一步。

4. 撤 步
前（後）腳退半步。

5. 跳 步
前腳蹬地跳起，後腳前擺落地。

6. 扣 步
上步落地時腳尖內扣，與後腳成八字。

7. 擺 步
上步落地時腳尖外擺，與後腳成八字。

8. 跟 步
後腳向前跟進半步。

9. 碾 步
以腳跟為軸，腳尖外展或內扣；或以腳掌為軸，腳跟外展。

【要領】

上步時，腳跟先著地，然後再過渡到全腳著地。後退時，前腳掌先著地，不可一下全腳著地。兩腳距離和跨度要因人而異，重心移動要平穩，步伐要輕靈，腳掌和腳跟碾度要適宜順遂。

2. Steps or Foot Movement

(1) Forward Step（Shang Bu）

The back foot takes a step forward.

(2) Moving Step（Huo Bu）

Keep the front foot moving during the movement.

(3) Backward Step（Tui Bu）

The front foot takes a step backward.

(4) Withdraw Step（Che Bu）

The front（or back）foot takes a half step backward.

(5) Jump Step（Tiao Bu）

The front foot jumps up and the back foot swings forward and lands on the ground.

(6) Toes in Step（Kou Bu）

Step forward with one foot. When the foot is placed on the ground, turn the toes inward to form a "/ \" shape with the back foot.

(7) Toes out Step（Bai Bu）

Step forward with one foot. When the foot is placed on the

ground, turn the toes outward to form a "\ /" shape with the back foot.

(8) Follow up Step (Gen Bu)

The back foot follows the front foot by half a step.

(9) Pivoting Step (Nian Bu)

Pivoting on the heel, turn the toes either inward or outward depending on the movement. Or, pivot on the forefoot and turn the heel outward or inward.

Key Points

When stepping forward, the heel touches the ground first, and then the entire foot is placed on the ground. When stepping backward, the forefoot touches the ground first. Avoid placing the whole foot on the ground at once. The distance between the feet should depend on the individual. The weight should be shifted steadily. The step should be flexible, and the pivoting movement of the heel or forefoot should be comfortable and smooth.

第三節　身型、身法與眼法

Section 3　Body Posture, Body Movements and Eyes

一、身　型

1. 頭
向上虛虛領起，下頜微微內收，不可偏歪和搖擺。

2. 頸
自然豎直，肌肉不可緊張。

3. 肩
保持鬆沉，不可聳肩，也不可前扣後張。

4. 肘
自然下墜，不可僵挺、外揚、掀翻。

5. 胸
舒鬆自然，不要外挺、內縮。

6. 背
自然放鬆，舒展拔伸，不可弓背。

7. 腰
自然放鬆，不後弓，不前挺，運轉靈活，以腰為軸，帶動四肢。

8. 脊

保持正直，不可左右歪斜、前挺後弓。

9. 臀、胯

臀要收斂，不可凸臀；胯要鬆、沉、縮、正，不可左右歪扭。

10. 膝

伸屈柔和自然。

1. Body Posture

(1) Head

Upright, do not lean or swing. The chin is tucked in slightly.

(2) Neck

Naturally upright and muscle relaxed.

(3) Shoulders

Maintain relaxed and sunk. Do not lift them up or push forward or stretch backward.

(4) Elbows

Sunken naturally. Do not be rigid or turned outward.

(5) Chest

Naturally relaxed. Avoid straightened or tucked.

(6) Back

Naturally relaxed. Upright and stretched. Do not stoop.

(7) Waist

Naturally relaxed. Do not be bent. Used as the axle of the

body and limbs.

(8) Spine

Maintained upright naturally. Do not lean in any direction.

(9) Buttocks and Hips

Pulled in. Maintained upright. The hips should be relaxed, sunken, tucked in, and upright.

(10) Knees

Extended or bent gently and naturally.

二、身　法

　　身法要求端正自然，不偏不倚，舒展大方，旋轉靈活；忌僵滯、浮軟，忽起忽落；以腰為軸，帶動四肢，完整貫穿。

2. Body Technique

The whole body is naturally upright, stretched, flexible, and comfortable. Avoid being rigid or too soft. Use the waist as the axle to lead the limbs and unify the whole body's motions.

三、眼　法

　　定勢時，眼看前方或劍；轉換時，應勢動神隨，神態自然。

3. Eye Technique

As each movement is finished, look ahead or at the sword

or at the Sword Fingers. When connecting movements, eyes follow the hands or the sword with a natural expression.

第四節　劍　法
Section 4　Sword Techniques

太極劍法通常有20多種，在這套32式太極劍中，主要有13種劍法，下面做簡要介紹。

1. 點 劍
立劍，提腕，使劍尖由上向下點擊，臂自然伸直，力達劍尖下鋒。

【要領】
手腕上提前送力達劍尖，手心鬆空。

There are generally more than 20 types of sword techniques. 13 of them are used in this form.

(1) Pointing Down (Dian Jian)
Hold the sword, edge up. Raise the wrist, and let the tip of the sword point down. Stretch the arm naturally and deliver the force to the lower edge.

Key Points
Force is delivered from the wrist to the tip of the sword. The hand is loose. Hold the handle with the fingers.

2. 刺 劍

　　立劍或平劍，向前直出為刺，勁達劍尖，臂與劍成一線，劍尖與胸平為平刺；劍尖高與頭平為上刺；劍尖與膝平為下刺；臂內旋，手心向外，劍經肩上側向前下（上）方立劍刺出為探刺。

【要領】

　　無論哪種刺劍，均應力貫劍尖。通常為墊把握劍。

(2) Thrust (Ci Jian)

Hold the sword with the blade flat or an edge up, and thrust it forward with force delivered to the tip, the arm and the sword in one line. When the tip is at chest level, it is called a Level Thrust(Ping Ci); when the tip is at head level, it is called an Up Thrust (Shang Ci); the tip at knee level is called a Down Thrust(Xia Ci). Lean and Thrust(Tan Ci): turn the arm inward, palm facing outward; thrust the sword to the lower or upper front, along or above the shoulders.

Key Points

Whatever the type of thrust, the force should be delivered to the tip of the sword. Underlying Gripping is used here.

3. 劈 劍

　　立劍，自上而下為劈，力達劍身，臂與劍成一直線。掄劈劍須將劍掄一立圓，然後向前下劈。劍身與胸平為平劈劍；劍身斜向下，劍尖與膝平為下劈劍。

【要領】

劈劍時，劍身一定保持立劍，手緊握劍柄。

(3) Chop (Pi Jian)

Hold the sword, edge up. Chop down with the force on the blade. The arm and the sword are aligned. The Swing and Chop (Lun Pi) is to swing the sword in a vertical circle with the shoulder acting as an axle, and cleave it down in front of the body. The Level Chop (Ping Pi) is to chop down to the chest level. The Downward Chop (Xia Pi) is done by cleaving, with the blade tilting down and the tip at knee level.

Key Points

When chopping, keep the edge of the sword facing up, and hold the handle tightly.

4. 掃 劍

平劍，向左或右平擺，擺幅大於90°，劍由低到高，高點在腰胸之間，勁貫劍刃。

【要領】

劍身起動貼地，以腰帶劍，以劍柄領劍身，劍身水平狀走圓弧。

(4) Sweep (Sao Jian)

Hold the sword, with blade flat. Sweep it to the upper left or the upper right over 90°, the highest point at the level between the waist and chest. The force is concentrated on the edge of the sword.

Key Points

Start with the sword near the ground, and let the waist lead the sword and the handle lead the blade. Move the sword in an arc.

5. 帶 劍

平劍，由前向左或右屈臂回抽為帶，腕高不過胸，劍尖斜向前，勁貫劍身中後部。

【要領】

帶劍時屈臂回抽要明顯，肩沉、肘墜、腕沉，下肢穩定。

(5) Withdraw (Dai Jian)

Hold the sword, with blade flat. Draw the sword back from the front to the left (or right) by bending the arm. The wrist is lower than the chest and the tip points diagonally forward. Deliver the force to the lower part of the sword.

Key Points

When drawing back the sword, bend the arm forcefully.

Sink the shoulders, the elbows and the wrists. Keep the lower limbs steady.

6. 撩 劍

立劍，由下向前上方為撩，力達劍身前部。正撩劍前臂外旋，手心向上，貼身弧形撩起；反撩劍前臂內旋，手心向外，貼身弧形撩起。

【要領】

無論是正撩或反撩，劍要走立圓，握劍之手在無名指與小指用力。

（6）Upward Slice（Liao Jian）

Hold the sword with the edge up. Wield the sword up in an arc with force going to the front part of the blade. Slicing Straight Up: turn the forearm outward until the palm faces upward, slicing up close to the body in an arc. Slicing Up, Towards the Back: turn the forearm inward until the palm faces outward, slicing up close to the body in an arc.

Key Points

Wield the sword in a vertical circle. Control the sword mainly with the ring finger and little finger.

7. 捧 劍

兩手心翻轉向上，由兩側向胸前結合，左手劍指或掌捧於右手背下，劍尖向前，略高於腕。

【要領】

捧劍兩手不可距胸過近，勁要從下向上捧托，注意沉肩、墜肘。

(7) Holding Sword with Both Hands（Peng Jian）

The two palms turn upward and join together in front of the chest, left hand cradling the right hand. The tip of the sword points forward and slightly higher than the wrist.

Key Points

When holding the sword, the hands shouldn't be too close to the chest. The sword is supported by an upward force. Sink the shoulders and elbows.

8. 攔 劍

攔劍分左攔劍和右攔劍。立劍，臂內旋，由左下向右前方斜出，腕與頭同高，劍尖向左前下，勁貫劍前刃為右攔劍。左攔劍與右攔劍動作相反，要領一致。

【要領】

攔劍是一種防守性劍法，其勁力點在劍下刃，手臂之內旋、外旋要與劍的運行協調配合，定勢時劍尖要對準身體中線。

(8) Parry（Lan Jian）

There is a Left Parry and a Right Parry. Right Parry: Hold

the sword edge up, turn the arm inward and move the sword from the lower left to the front right until the wrist is at the level of the head. The tip of the sword points down to the lower front, force going through the front edge of the sword. The Left Parry is the same in the opposite direction.

Key Points

Parrying is a technique used for defense. The force is on the lower edge of the sword. Turn the arm inward or outward in co-ordination with the moving sword. When it is completed, the tip of the sword should align with the centre of one's body.

9. 截 劍

劍由左向右、向下按落為截，勁達劍身下刃。

【要領】

力注劍刃，要有下按之意，為防守性劍法。

(9) Intercepting (Jie Jian)

Move the sword to the lower left or the lower right, with force going to the lower edge of the blade.

Key Points

Deliver the force onto the edge of the sword with the intention of pressing down. This is a technique for defense.

10. 掛 劍

立劍，劍尖由前向下向同側或異側貼身掛出，勁貫劍身前部。

【要領】

握劍手腕稍內扣，注意劍要貼身。

(10) Stabbing Back（Gua Jian）

Hold the sword, edge up. The tip of the sword goes behind the body from either side. The force is on the front part of the blade.

Key Points

Turn the hand holding the sword slightly inward. Stab the sword backward, close to the body.

11. 抹 劍

平劍，劍從一側經體前弧形向另一側抽帶為抹，高與胸平，劍尖向異側前方，勁達劍身。

【要領】

劍身與地面平行，以腰帶動圓弧平抹。

(11) Slide（Mo Jian）

Hold the sword, with blade flat. Wield the sword in an arc from one side of the body to the other and across the front. The blade is at the level of the chest, the tip of the sword pointing the opposite direction. Deliver the force to the blade.

Key Points

Keep the sword blade parallel to the ground. The waist leads the sword to move in an arc.

12. 削 劍

平劍，自異側下方經胸前向同側上方斜出為削。手心斜向上，劍尖略高於頭。

【要領】

墊把握劍，力達劍刃，臂與劍成一直線。

(12) Peel（Xiao Jian）

Hold the sword, with blade flat. Wield the sword upward diagonally from the other side of the body to the side of the hand holding the sword, across the chest. The palm is facing diagonally up and the tip of the sword is slightly above the head.

Key Points

Hold the sword in Underlying Gripping, force reaching the edge. The arm is aligned with the sword.

13. 架（托）劍

立劍，手心向外，由下向右上方為架，劍高過頭，劍身橫直，勁貫劍身中部。立劍，手心向裏，由下向上為托，腕與頭平，勁貫全身中部，劍身橫直。

【要領】

托劍劍身不要擋住眼睛，通常架劍與托劍合稱架托劍。

(13) Holding Up and Lifting (Jia Jian and Tuo Jian)

Holding Up Sword: hold the sword with the edge up. Raise the sword up above the head, with the palm facing outward. The blade of the sword is horizontal, and the force is on the middle part of the sword. Lifting Sword: hold the sword with edge up; lift the sword upward to head level with the palm facing inward. The wrist at head level, the sword blade is horizontal, and the force on the middle part of the sword.

Key Points

When lifting the sword, avoid blocking the sight. Usually holding up a sword and lifting a sword together is called "Holding Up and Lifting".

第三章

32式太極劍套路詳解

Chapter 3　Movement Of 32-form Tai Chi Sword

第一節 32式太極劍套路劍譜

Section 1 List of the 32-form Tai Chi Sword Movements

預備式（無極式）

起式（三環套月）

第一組

一、併步點劍（金雞啄米）

二、獨立反刺（大魁星）

三、仆步橫掃（燕子抄水）

四、向右平帶（右攔掃）

五、向左平帶（左攔掃）

六、獨立掄劈（哪吒探海）

七、退步回抽（懷中抱月）

八、獨立上刺（宿鳥投林）

第二組

九、虛步下截（烏龍擺尾）

十、左弓步刺（青龍出水）

十一、轉身斜帶（風捲荷葉）

十二、縮身斜帶（獅子搖頭）

十三、提膝捧劍（虎抱頭）

十四、跳步平刺（野馬跳澗）

十五、左虛步撩（小魁星）

十六、右弓步撩（水中撈月）

第三組

十七、轉身回抽（射雁式）

十八、併步平刺（白猿獻果）

十九、左弓步攔（迎風撣塵①）

二十、右弓步攔（迎風撣塵②）

二十一、左弓步攔（迎風撣塵③）

二十二、進步反刺（順水推舟）

二十三、反身回劈（流星趕月）

二十四、虛步點劍（燕子銜泥）

第四組

二十五、獨立平托（挑簾式）

二十六、弓步掛劈（左車輪）

二十七、虛步掄劈（右車輪）

二十八、撤步反擊（大鵬展翅）

二十九、進步平刺（烏龍攪柱）

三十、丁步回抽（懷中抱月）

三十一、旋轉平抹（風掃梅花）

三十二、弓步直刺（指南針）

收式（抱劍歸原）

Preparation（Wu Ji Form）

Commencing（Three Rings Around the Moon）

Group 1

1. Point Sword with Feet Together（Golden Cock Pecks Rice）

2. Stand on One Leg and Thrust（The Great Dipper）

3. Sweep Sword in Crouch Step（The Swallow Skims the Water）

4. Withdraw Sword to the Right（Block and Sweep to the Right）

5. Withdraw Sword to the Left（Block and Sweep to the Left）

6. Swing and Chop with One Leg Standing（Nézhā Explores the Sea）

7. Step Back and Withdraw Sword（Embrace the Moon）

8. Thrust Upward with One Leg Standing（Bird Returns to Tree at Dusk）

Group 2

9. Intercept Downward with Empty Step (Black Dragon Whips Tail)

10. Thrust in Left Bow Step (Green Dragon Emerges from Water)

11. Turn Body and Withdraw Sword Diagonally (Wind Blows Lotus Leaves)

12. Retreat and Withdraw Sword (Lion Shakes its Mane)

13. Lift Knee and Hold Sword with Both Hands (Tiger Holds its Head)

14. Hop and Thrust Sword with Blade Flat (Wild Horse Leaps Over Creek)

15. Slice Sword Upward with Left Empty Stance (The Little Dipper)

16. Slice Sword Upward with Right Bow Step (Scoop the Moon from Bottom of Sea)

Group 3

17. Turn Around and Withdraw Sword (Shooting Wild Goose)

18. Thrust with Feet Together (White Ape Offers Fruit)

19. Parry in Left Bow Stance (Dusting in the Wind①)

20. Parry in Right Bow Stance (Dusting in the Wind②)

21. Parry in Left Bow Stance (Dusting in the Wind③)

22. Step Forward and Plunge Backward (Pushing the Boat with Current)

23. Turn Around to Chop (The Comet Chases the Moon)

24. Point Sword in Empty Stance (Swallow Picks up Mud with its Beak)

Group 4

25. Level Sword and Stand on One Leg (Lift Door Curtain)

26. Wheeling Chop in Right Bow Step (Left Wheeling)

27. Swing Chop in Right Empty Step (Right Wheeling)

28. Step Back to Strike Backward (Phoenix Spreads its Wings)

29. Step Forward to Thrust (Black Dragon Coils Around Pole)

30. Withdraw Sword in T- Step (Holding the Moon)

31. Turn Body and Slide Sword (Wind Sweeps and Plum Blossoms)

32. Thrust forward in Bow Step (Compass)

Closing (Return the Sword to Its Original Position)

第二節　32式太極劍套路動作說明

Section 2　32-form Tai Chi Sword Detail Explanation Step by Step

預備式（無極式）

1. 併步持劍

　　面向正南，兩腳並立，身體正直，兩臂自然下垂於身體兩側，左手持劍，劍身豎直，劍尖向上，與身體平行。右手掌心向裏，中指輕輕貼於大腿外側，眼平視前方（圖3-1）。

圖3-1

53

Preparation（Wu Ji Form）

(1) Hold Sword and Feet Together

Face south with feet together, the body upright and the arms naturally hanging down at the sides of the body. The left hand holds the sword with the blade upright, tip pointing up and parallel to the body. The palm of the right hand faces inward with the middle finger slightly touching the outside of the leg. Look ahead（Figure 3-1）.

2. 持劍開步

重心移向右腳，左腳跟離地，再提起左腳向左橫跨半步，腳尖先點地，再慢慢全腳踏實，與肩同寬，重心移至兩腳。右手變為劍指，兩臂內旋，兩手心向後，距離身體10公分，目視前方。

【要領】

（1）頭頸自然豎直，下頜微收，上體中正自然，不挺胸不收腹，肩臂應自然鬆沉。劍刃不要觸及身體，精神貫注。

（2）心舒體鬆，暗合無極狀態，調整身心。

（3）持劍開步要點起點落，動作勻緩沉穩。

【意念】

（1）意想全身，按太極拳、劍要領，做到虛領頂勁，含胸拔背，鬆腰斂臀，尾閭中正。

（2）思想集中，平心靜氣，神情舒展，氣沉丹田，做腹式深呼吸。

(2) Hold Sword and Step Aside

While the weight shifts to the right foot, the left heel moves off the ground. Lift the left foot and move to the left in a half step; first only the toes touch the ground, and then the whole foot is placed down solidly, feet apart at shoulder width. At the same time, shift the weight between the legs. The right hand forms the Sword Fingers. The arms turn inwards and the palms face backward, about 10 cm from the body. Eyes look ahead.

Key Points

（1）Keep the head and the upper body naturally upright; the chin is tucked in slightly. Do not stiffen the chest or suck in the abdomen. The shoulders are naturally relaxed and sunken. Avoid touching the body with the edge of the sword. The mind is focused.

（2）Keep the mind peaceful and the body relaxed in a quiet and comfortable state to adjust the body and mind.

（3）When stepping, lift the heel first and place the toes on the floor first. Move slowly and stably.

Keep in Mind

（1）The entire body follows the principle of Tai Chi Chuan

and Sword: keeping the head naturally upright; pull the chest in and stretch the back; relax the waist and the hips. Keep the tail bone at the centre.

(2) Keep the mind concentrated. Mood is calm and peaceful. Sink the energy to the abdomen. Breathe through the abdomen.

起 式（三環套月）

1. 兩臂前舉

兩臂慢慢向前上平舉，高與肩平，手心向下，眼看前方（圖3-2）。

【要領】

（1）兩臂前平舉時，肩要自然放鬆，不要用力，不可聳肩，兩手寬度不要超過兩肩。

（2）劍身在左臂下貼緊左前臂，劍首向前，劍尖不可下垂。

【意念】

兩臂前平舉時，兩手與命門對拉，頭上領、肩下沉，做深吸氣。

Commencing（Three Rings Around the Moon）

(1) Raise Arms Forward

Raise the arms forward slowly to the shoulder height, palms facing down. Eyes look ahead (Figure 3-2).

Key Points

(1) When raising the arms, the shoulders should be relaxed. Do not put the force on the shoulders or raise them up. The hands should be apart no more than shoulder's width.

(2) The blade of the sword attaches closely to the left forearm, the pommel of the sword pointing forward. Keep the sword leveled.

Keep in Mind

When raising the arms forward, push the hands and the "Ming Men" in opposite directions. ("Ming Men" is acupuncture point, which is in the middle of the waist) Draw the head up and sink the shoulders. Breathe deeply.

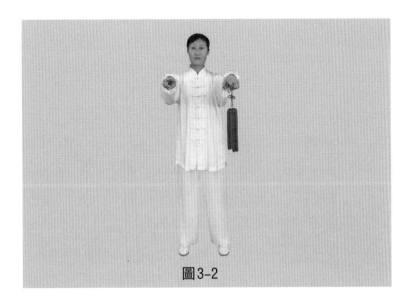

圖3-2

2.轉體擺臂

上體略向右轉，身體重心移於右腿，屈膝下蹲，隨後左腳提起收至右腳內側。同時，右劍指邊翻轉邊由體前下落，經腹前弧線向右上舉，手心向上；左手持劍經面前屈肘落於右肩前，手心向下，劍平置於胸前，眼看劍指（圖3-3）。

【要領】

（1）重心移於右腿平穩後，再收左腳，腳尖不可點地。

（2）左手持劍畫弧及劍指畫弧平舉時，肩部要放鬆，上體保持正直，不可向右傾。

【意念】

右側腰腎放鬆，氣下沉，以腰帶手擺臂，呼氣配合。

(2) Turn Body and Swing Arm

Turn the upper body to the right slightly and shift the weight onto the right leg. Bend the knee to a half squat. Lift the left foot and move it beside the right foot. Meanwhile, the right Sword Fingers turn over and fall down in front of the body, and then are raised in an arc from the abdomen to the upper right, palm facing up. The left hand holds the sword and moves to the right shoulder by bending the arm, the palm facing down and the sword maintained leveled in front of the chest. Eyes follow the Sword Fingers (Figure 3-3).

Key Points

(1) Bring the left foot in after shifting the weight onto the right foot. Do not place the toes on the ground.

(2) When the hand is holding the sword or the Sword Fingers are moving in an arc, relax the shoulders. Keep the upper body upright; do not lean to the left or right.

Keep in Mind

Relax the right side of the waist. Sink the energy. The waist leads the arms and hands to move. Exhale in co-ordination.

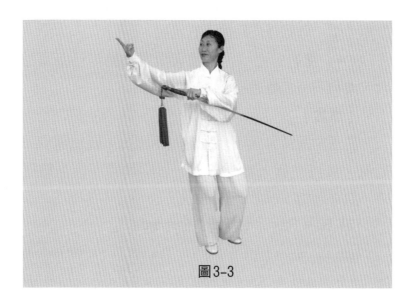

圖3-3

3. 弓步前指

上體左轉，左腳向左前方邁出，屈膝前弓；右腿自然伸直，右腳跟後碾，成左弓步。同時，左手持劍經體前向左下方摟至左胯旁，劍豎直立於左前臂後，劍尖向上；右臂屈肘，劍指經右耳旁隨轉體向前指出，指尖自然斜向上，高與眼平，眼看劍指（圖3-4）。

【要領】

（1）左腳向左前邁出時，先腳跟著地，隨重心前移左腿屈膝前弓，全腳慢慢踏實，腳尖向前，膝部不可超過腳尖。

（2）右腿自然伸直時以右腳尖為軸，腳跟碾動要適宜。

（3）弓步時，兩腳橫向距離在20公分左右。因是拗弓步，兩腳橫向距離不宜過寬。

（4）轉體、上步、弓腿與兩臂的動作要協調配合，柔和不僵，輕靈平穩。

【意念】

注意左側腰腎氣下沉，鬆左側腰胯，圓襠開步，吸氣，氣貫左腳，襠走下弧，鬆腰轉體，後腳蹬碾時，勁貫劍指，呼氣定勢。

(3) Bow Step and Point Forward

Turn the upper body to the left. The left foot steps towards the left front and the knee is bent. Extend the right leg straight naturally, pivoting on the forefoot backward to form a Left Bow Step. At the same time, move the left hand, which is holding the sword, across the body down to the left hip, with the sword erecting behind the left forearm and the tip facing up. Bend the right arm, and along with the turning body, the Sword Fingers move forward to the side of ear, finger tip at eye-level and pointing diagonally upwards. The eyes look at the Sword Fingers (Figure 3-4).

Key Points

(1) While the left foot steps towards the front left, the heel touches the ground first; shift the weight onto the left leg and bend the leg forward and then place the entire foot on the ground

圖3-4

solidly, toes pointing forward. Do not bend the knee beyond the toes.

(2) Pivoting on the right forefoot, swing the heel accordingly and extend the right leg straight naturally.

(3) The distance between the parallel lines on which the feet are placed is about 20cm. As this Bow Step is a Side Bow Step, the distance should not be too great.

(4) The moving of the body, feet and arms should co-ordinate with each other gently, flexibly and stably.

Keep in Mind

Relax and sink the energy on the left side of the waist. Step forward with knees bent outward, turn the body with relaxed waist, and inhale with the energy going through the left foot. When pivoting on the right foot, deliver the energy to the Sword Fingers. Exhale when the movement is completed.

4. 坐盤展臂

身體右轉，左臂屈肘上提，左手持劍手心向下，經胸前從右手上穿出；右劍指翻轉手心向上，並慢慢下落經腰間擺至身體右側，手心向上，兩臂左右平展。同時，右腳提起向前蓋步橫落，腳尖外撇，兩腿交叉，膝關節前後相抵；左腳跟掀起，重心稍下降成半坐盤姿勢，眼看劍指（圖3-5）。

【要領】

（1）兩手體前交錯時，左手持劍穿出，劍首在前，不可屈肘橫劍推出。

（2）右手後撤要經腹前畫弧後展，不可向後豎肩直抽，應與上體右轉協調一致。

（3）蓋步坐盤動作要輕靈、平穩，不可搶步、突然坐胯，不要成全坐盤。

（4）左手持劍穿出時，左前臂內旋，劍貼於臂後。

【意念】

（1）注意氣沉於左腳上，收左胯。蓋步時頭上領，尾閭中正，呼氣沉肩。

圖3-5

（2）劍首前穿，勁貫劍首，有劍首攻擊之意。

(4) Stretch Arms and Squat Low with Crossed-Legs

Turn the body to the right. Bend the left arm and raise it up. The left hand holds the sword with the palm facing down and moves above the right hand in front of the body. The right Sword Fingers turn over with the palm facing up and move down slowly along the waist to the right side of the body. The two arms are stretched up to shoulder level. At the same time, lift the right foot and place it ahead of the left foot to form Crossover Step, toes pointing outward. The left knee is attached to the inside of the right knees. Lift the left heel off the ground and lower the weight to form a low squat with legs crossed. The eyes look at the sword finger (Figure 3-5).

Key Points

（1）When the two hands cross each other in front of the body, move the left hand over the right hand with the pommel of the sword pointing forward. Do not bend the elbow to push the sword across.

（2）Co-ordinating with the turning body, draw back the right hand in an arc in front of the abdomen. Do not pull it back straight.

（3）The action of cross-legged sitting should be light and stable. Avoid being abrupt, and also avoid sitting completely.

（4）When the left hand pushes the sword forward, rotate the left forearm inward, the sword clinging to the back of the forearm.

Keep in Mind

（1）Sink the energy onto the left foot. Draw the left hip in. Keep one's head and spine upright. Sink the shoulders with exhaling.

（2）Thrust the pommel of the sword forward. Deliver the force to the pommel with the intention of offense.

5. 弓步接劍

重心慢慢提起，落於右腳，左腳提起上步屈膝，腳尖向前，右腿自然伸直成左弓步。同時，上體左轉，右手劍指經頭右上方向前弧形落於劍柄，準備接劍，眼看前方（圖3-6）。

【要領】

（1）動作時要先提左腳上步，右臂上舉，然後屈膝弓腿，劍指向前下落，兩肩放鬆，兩臂自然舒伸，上體保持正直。

（2）劍指下落後亦可成右掌附於劍柄。

（3）兩腳橫向距離為20～30公分，不可成一線步或麻花步型。

【意念】

（1）左腳上步時要縮住左胯根，襠走下弧。上

（2）右腳蹬碾時，勁上傳於右手接劍，以吸氣配合。

(5) Hand Over the Sword in Bow Step

Raise the weight and shift it onto the right foot. Lift the left foot to step forward and bend the leg, toes pointing forward. Extend the right leg naturally straight to form Left Bow Step. Meanwhile, turn the upper body to the left. The right Sword Fingers draw an arc from the upper right of the head down to the handle of the sword, ready to take over the sword. Eyes look ahead (Figure 3–6).

圖3-6

Key Points

（1）In this movement, lift the left foot and raise the right arm first, then bend the knee and move down the Sword Fingers. Keep the shoulders relaxed, arms naturally extended and the upper body upright.

（2）After falling down, the Sword Fingers can also turn into an open palm to rest on the handle of the sword.

（3）The feet rest on two parallel lines which are apart about 20–30cm. The feet should neither be on one line nor be crossed.

Keep in Mind

（1）When the left foot steps forward, the left hipbone should be drawn in and the crotch moves in a downward arc. Avoid the upper body moving up or down. Sink the energy down to the left foot.

（2）When the right foot steps and grinds on the ground, deliver the force to the right hand and take over the sword, inhaling.

第一組

一、併步點劍（金雞啄米）

左手食指向中指一側靠攏，右手鬆開劍指，虎口對著護手，握住劍柄，將劍接換過來，而後腕關節繞環，使劍在身體左側畫一立圓，劍尖向前下點出，力達劍尖，左手變成劍指，附於右手腕部。同時，右腳向左腳靠攏成併步，身體半蹲，眼看劍尖（圖3-7）。

【要領】

（1）劍身向前環繞時，兩臂要向下壓，不可高舉。

（2）點劍時，臂先沉肘屈收，再提腕前送，使劍尖由上向下點啄，力達劍尖。點劍要以拇指、無名指和小指著力，持劍要鬆活。

（3）兩腳併步不宜過緊，兩腳全腳掌著地，兩腿屈膝半蹲，重心以左腳為主，不可成丁步，上體保持正直。

【意念】

意想縮胯收腳，勁貫劍尖，點劍呼氣送勁。

Group 1

1. Point Sword with Feet Together

（Golden Cock　Pecks Rice）

Move the left index finger close to the middle finger. The right hand changes from Sword Fingers into an open palm and grasps the hilt of the sword with the "tiger mouth" against the guard. After taking the sword over, the right hand holds the sword and draws a vertical ellipse at the left side of the body by turning the wrist. Then point the sword to the lower front, force reaching the tip. At this time, the left hand forms Sword Fingers and rests on the right wrist. Meanwhile, move the right foot close to the left foot and bend the knees. Eyes look at the tip of the sword (Figure 3-7).

Key Points

(1) When drawing the ellipse with the sword, push the arms down. Don't raise them.

(2) When pointing the sword down, sink the elbow and bend the arm first, and then lift the wrist forward; stab the tip downward and deliver the force to it. The sword is mainly controlled by the thumb, the third finger and the little finger. Hold

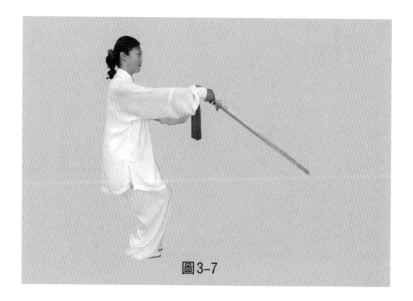

圖3-7

the sword loosely and flexibly.

(3) The feet shouldn't be too close to each other. The feet touch the ground fully and the knees are bent to a half squat. The weight is mainly on the left foot. The feet should not form a T-step. Keep the upper body upright.

Keep in Mind

Focus the mind on: pulling the hips in and bring the foot in. Delivering the force to the tip, exhaling.

二、獨立反刺（大魁星）

1. 撤步抽劍

右腳向右後方撤步，隨即上體後移。右手持劍抽回至右腹前，劍斜置於體前，劍尖向前上；左手劍指附於右手腕隨劍回抽，眼看劍尖（圖3-8）。

【要領】

（1）右腳後撤，腳前掌先著地，隨即右腿屈膝，右腳慢慢踏實，重心移至右腳。右腳後撤落點要偏右後方。右腳落地時，腳尖外撇大約60°。

（2）右手持劍抽撤時，落臂沉腕，劍尖自然抬起，上體保持中正，不可搖晃。

【意念】

氣下沉，背後倚撤步，上體中正，勁貫劍下刃，吸氣配合。

2. Stand on One Leg and Thrust(The Great Dipper)

(1) Step Backward and Pull Sword

The right foot steps to the right back, and move the upper body backward. The right hand holds the sword and pulls it back in the right front of the abdomen, the sword laid obliquely before the body and the tip pointing to the upper front. The left fingers, attaching on the wrist of the right hand, follow the sword. Eyes look at the tip (Figure 3-8).

Key Points

(1) Bring the right foot back with only the forefoot touching the ground first and then bend the knee. Placing the right foot on the ground firmly and slowly, the weight shifts to the

圖3-8

right foot. Place the right foot towards the right behind the body, and the toes turn outwards about 60°.

(2) When the right hand is pulling back the sword, sink the arm and the wrist; tilt the tip of the sword up naturally. Keep the upper body upright without swinging.

Keep in Mind

When moving back, breathe through the abdomen; draw your back backward. Keep the upper body upright; deliver the force to the lower edge of the sword; inhale in co-ordination.

2. 收腳挑劍

上體向右後轉，隨之左腳收至右腳內側，腳尖點地。同時，右手持劍繼續反手抽撩至右後方，然後右臂外旋，右腕下沉，使劍尖上挑，劍身立於身體右側；左手劍指隨劍撤於右上臂內側，眼看劍尖（圖3-9）。

【要領】

（1）右腳原地不動踏實，保持上體不起伏。

（2）上體右轉帶動右腕翻轉下沉，上挑劍的動作要連貫自然，不可掀肩，上體保持正直。

（3）劍上挑時，握劍要鬆活，不可死握，劍在拇指和食指間運動，其餘三指鬆握，起輔助作用。

（4）眼要隨劍的運動轉動，目視劍尖。

【意念】

（1）腰氣下沉，鬆腰轉體呼氣，帶動劍身後撩。

（2）劍尖上挑時要縮胯、沉肩、屈腕、吸氣，勁注劍尖。

（2）Bring Foot in and Lift Sword

Turn the upper body to the right rear, and move the left foot beside the right foot with the toes touching the ground. At the same time, the right hand continues to wield the sword towards the right rear. Rotate the right arm outward and sink the right wrist to swing the tip up. At this point, the blade of the sword erects by the right side of the body, and the left fingers move down to the inside of the right upper arm. Eyes look at

圖3-9

the tip of the sword (Figure 3-9).

Key Points

(1) The right foot stands at the original place solidly. Do not move the upper body up or down.

(2) Upper body leads the right wrist turning over and sinking. The moving of the sword should be fluent; do not raise the shoulder. Keep the upper body upright.

(3) When swinging the sword up, hold the sword loosely and flexibly. The thumb and the index finger control the sword and the other three fingers assist it.

(4) Eyes follow the sword, looking at the tip.

Keep in Mind

(1) Sink the waist. Relax the waist. Turn the body to draw the sword back, exhaling to co-ordinate.

(2) When swinging up the sword, draw the hip in; sink the shoulder; bend the wrist; inhale. Deliver the force to the tip of the sword.

3. 提膝反刺

上體左轉，右腳踩穩，左膝提起，高與腰齊，成獨立步。同時，右手持劍由後漸漸上舉，經頭右側上方向前反手刺出，手心向外，力達劍尖；左手劍指經頷下隨轉體向前指出，高與眼平，眼看劍指（圖

3–10）。

【要領】

（1）右腿自然直立，不可硬挺。左膝儘量上提，腳面展平，腳尖下垂，小腿和腳微向裏扣護襠。

（2）上體正直，頂頭豎項，下頜內收，兩眼有神。

（3）左膝向正前，左肘左膝上下相對。適宜合襠，不要夾襠。

（4）反刺劍，劍身平，劍尖略低，由後向前刺出，不能做成架劍。

【意念】

（1）頭上領，氣下沉，上下對拉，尾閭對準腳跟。

圖3-10

（2）右胯跟縮住，氣下沉右腳下，保持重心穩定。勁貫劍尖，呼氣助力。

(3) Lift Knee and Stab in Backhand

Turn the upper body to the left. Place the right foot on the ground firmly. Raise the left knee at waist level to form an Independent Step. At the same time, raise the sword gradually past the upper right side of the head and stab forward, palm facing outward and delivering the force to the tip. The left Sword Fingers follow the body, past underside of the chin and point forward at the height of the eyes. The eyes look at the Sword Fingers (Figure 3-10).

Key Points

(1) The right leg stands naturally straight; do not be rigid. Raise the left knee as high as possible, the foot stretched, toes pointing downward. Draw the lower leg and foot inward to protect the crotch.

(2) Keep the upper body upright; draw the head and neck up. Tuck the chin in. Eyes are sharp.

(3) Bend the left knee forward. The left elbow is above the left knee. Push thighs together, but not too tightly.

(4) Stab the sword in backhand with the blade flat, the tip slightly down. Stab from the back to the front. Don't form a Holding Up posture (Jia Jian).

Keep in Mind

(1) Draw the head up. The energy(Qi) flows down. Push the upper body and lower body in the opposite directions. The tail bone is over the right heel.

(2) Pull the base of the right hip in. The energy goes to the right foot. Keep the weight steady. Deliver the force to the tip of sword; exhale to increase the power.

三、仆步橫掃（燕子抄水）

1. 撤步劈劍

上體右後轉，劍隨轉體向右後方平劈，右臂與劍平直一線，左劍指落於右腕部。在轉體同時，右腿屈膝，左腿向左後（東北向）撤步，左腿自然伸直，成右側弓步，眼看劍尖（圖3-11）。

【要領】

（1）左腿撤步時，右腳方向不動，為側弓步，上體重心主要由右腿承擔。

（2）劍劈向西南，左腿撤步在東北，劍與左腿方向相反。

【意念】

（1）鬆右膝右胯吸氣下沉，身體下降。

（2）身體下降，同時鬆肩帶動劍由上而下劈出，呼氣助力，勁貫劍下刃。

3. Sweep Sword in Crouch Step

(The Swallow Skims the Water)

(1) Step Backward and Chop

Turn the upper body to the right and chop, the sword aligned with the right arm. Place the left Sword Fingers on the right wrist. As the body is turning, bend the right knee and bring the left leg towards the left back (north-east). Extend the left leg naturally to form a right Side Bow Step. Eyes look at the tip of the sword (Figure 3-11).

Key Points

(1) When the left foot is stepping back, keep the right leg at the original place. The weight is mainly on the right leg.

圖3-11

（2）The sword splits to the southwest and the left leg steps towards the northeast, so they are in opposite directions.

Keep in Mind

（1）Relax the right hip and knee; inhale. Lower the upper body.

（2）While the body is lowered, relax the shoulders and split the sword downward. Deliver the force to the lower edge of the sword. Exhale to increase the power.

2. 仆步横掃

上體左轉，左劍指經體前順左肋間反抽，並向上方弧線上舉，手心斜向上；右手持劍翻轉，手心向上，平劍自右後方向下、向左前方弧線平掃。同時，右腿屈蹲成半仆步，重心逐漸左移，左腳外撇，左腿屈弓，右腳尖內扣，右腿自然伸直，成左弓步，劍與胸同高，眼看劍尖（圖3-12）。

【要領】

（1）上體重心左移時，左腳尖盡力外撇，腳尖向東偏北；右腳尖裏扣，成左弓步，使步型順遂。不可彎腰，上體保持正直。

（2）掃劍時，劍為平劍，力在劍前刃，劍先下落，再由低到高，平穩地向左掃去，右手停於左肋前，劍尖對準上體中線，高與胸平。

（3）左手劍指反插時，要在左肋處內旋向後下方伸出，再弧線向左上方舉起，左臂要撐圓，不可過屈、過直。

【意念】

開襠沉氣，襠走下弧，呼氣助力，勁注劍前刃，捲動而掃。

(2) Sweep Sword with Crouch Step

While the upper body turns to the left, pull the left Sword Fingers back along the left rib, across in front of the body, and then lift it up in an arc, palm facing diagonally up. The right hand turns over, palm facing up. Sweep the sword downward with blade flat from the right back, and then to the front left.

圖3-12

Meanwhile, bend the right knee to a half Crouch Step and shift the weight to the left gradually. Turn the left foot outward and bend the leg. Turn the right foot inward and extend the leg naturally to form a left Bow Step. The sword is at chest level. Eyes look at the tip of the sword (Figure 3-12).

Key Points

(1) When shifting the weight to the left, turn the left toes outward as much as possible; make it point to the east and slightly northward. The right toes turn inward to form left Bow Step. Do not bend the upper body; keep it upright.

(2) When sweeping, the sword is leveled with force on the front edge. Move the sword first down, and then up, sweeping steadily to the left. The right hand stops before the left ribs, with the tip of the sword at chest level and the blade aligning with the centre of the upper body.

(3) When moving the left Sword Fingers back along the body, rotate it inward at the left ribs first and then to the lower back, and then lift it up to the upper left in an arc. The left arm is arched, but do not bend it too much or rigid.

Keep in Mind

Open the crotch; sink the energy (Qi); move the crotch in a downward arc. Deliver the force to the front edge of the sword, rolling and sweeping; exhale to increase the power.

四、向右平帶（右攔掃）

1. 收腳收劍

右腳提起收至左腳內側（腳尖不點地，初學者可點地穩定重心）。同時，右手持劍稍向內收至左小腹處，左劍指落於右腕部，眼看劍尖（圖3-13）。

【要領】

右手持劍屈臂回收，劍尖略高，劍尖保持在體前中線上，劍尖不可左擺。

【意念】

縮左胯，氣下沉；鬆右胯，右腳回收時以大腿帶小腿，吸氣配合。

4. Withdraw Sword to the Right

（Block and Sweep to the Right）

(1) Bring the Foot in and Withdraw Sword

Lift the right foot and place it beside of the left foot. (The toes do not touch the ground. The beginner can do so for the weight stabilization) Meanwhile, the right hand holds the sword and moves slightly inward to the left of the lower abdomen. Place the left Sword Fingers on the wrist of the right hand. Eyes look at the tip of the sword (Figure 3–13).

Key Points

Bend the right arm to withdraw the sword, the tip slightly

higher than the blade. Keep the tip aligned with the centre of the body; do not swing it to the left.

Keep in Mind

Pull the left hip in and sink the energy. Relax the right hip. The right thigh leads the lower leg and draws the foot in. Inhale.

2. 上步送劍

重心踩在左腳，右腳向右前方邁出一步，腳跟著地。同時，右手持劍向前外弧伸出，左劍指仍附於右腕部，眼看劍尖（圖3-14）。

【要領】

（1）上步方向在體前中線右側30°～45°之間。

（2）上體保持正直，不要彎腰凸臀。

圖3-13　　　　圖3-14

【意念】

呼氣落胯，氣由丹田向四肢擴散，勁貫劍尖。

(2) Step Forward to Send Sword

Shift the weight to the left foot. The right foot steps towards the right front, only the heel touching the ground. At the same time, move the sword forward in an arc. The left Sword Fingers still rest on the right wrist. Eyes look at the tip of the sword (Figure 3-14).

Key Points

(1) The right foot steps to the right front 30° to 45° in relation to the upper body.

(2) Keep the upper body upright. Do not bend the waist or push the buttocks out.

Keep in Mind

Sink the hip and exhale. The energy (Qi) from the abdomen goes to the limbs. Deliver the force to the tip of the sword.

3. 弓步右帶

重心向右腳移動，右腳踏實，成右弓步。右手持劍，手心翻轉向下，向右後方屈臂斜帶，左劍指仍附於右腕部，眼看劍尖（圖3-15）。

【要領】

（1）帶劍為平劍，由前向斜後方柔緩平穩地弧形回帶，力在劍刃，劍尖保持在體前中線附近，不可左右大幅擺動。

（2）屈臂帶劍與弓步要協調一致，同時配合上體微微右轉。

（3）帶劍要注意由前往後屈臂回帶，力點在劍刃上滑動，不要做成掛劍、掃劍。

【意念】

動作要連續，不可斷勁，劍回帶時要鬆腰沉氣，呼氣平穩。

(3) Bow Step and Withdraw Sword to Right

Shift the weight onto the right leg and place the right foot on the ground firmly to form a right Bow Step. The right hand

圖3–15

holds the sword and turns over with the palm facing down. Bend the arm to wield the sword towards the right back. The left Sword Fingers still rest on the right wrist. The eyes look at the sword tip (Figure 3–15).

Key Points

(1) Hold the sword with the blade flat. Draw the sword backward slowly and steadily in an arc, with force on the edge and the tip near the middle of the front of the body. Do not swing too much to the left or right.

(2) The bending arm withdrawing the sword should move in co-ordination with the Bow Step. At the same time, turn the upper body slightly to the right.

(3) Draw the sword backward by bending the arm, the force going along the edge. Do not mix up the movement with "Stabbing Back" and "Sweeping".

Keep in Mind

Move continuously. When drawing the sword back, relax the waist and sink the energy; breathe evenly.

五、向左平帶（左攔掃）

1. 收腳收劍

右手持劍屈臂後收至右小腹處。同時，左腳提起收至右腳內側（初習者腳尖可點地），眼看劍尖（圖

3-16）。

【要領】

與「向右平帶」動作1同，只是左右方向相反。

【意念】

與「向右平帶」動作1同。

5. Withdraw Sword to the Left

（Block and Sweep to the Left）

(1) Bring the Foot in and Withdraw Sword

Bend the right arm and draw the sword back to the right front of the lower abdomen. Meanwhile, raise the left foot and place it beside the right foot. (The toes don't touch the ground. The beginner can do so for stability) Eyes look at the tip of the

圖3-16

sword（Figure 3-16）.

Key Points

Key Points are the same as those for "Withdraw Sword to the Right（1）" in the opposite direction.

Keep in Mind

Notes are the same as those under "Keep in Mind" for "Withdraw Sword to the Right（1）".

2. 上步送劍

左腳向左前方上步，腳跟著地。右手持劍向前伸送，左劍指翻轉收至腰間，手心向上，眼看劍尖（圖3-17）。

圖3-17

【要領】

與「向右平帶」動作2同，只是左右方向相反。

【意念】

與「向右平帶」動作2同。

(2) Step Forward to Thrust Sword

The left foot steps towards the left front, only the heel touching the ground. At the same time, move the sword forward in an arc. The left Sword Fingers turn over and pull back to the left side of the waist, palm facing up. Eyes look at the tip of the sword (Figure 3–17).

Key Points

Key Points are the same as those for "Withdraw Sword to the Right(2)" in the opposite direction.

Keep in Mind

See "Keep in Mind" for "Withdraw Sword to the Right(2)".

3. 弓步左帶

右手持劍翻轉向左後方弧線平劍回帶至左肋前方，力在劍刃；左手劍指繼續向左上方畫弧舉至額頭左上方，手心斜向上。左腿前弓，重心前移，成左弓步，眼看劍尖（圖3–18）。

【要領】

除左手劍指畫弧上舉外，其餘與「向右平帶」動作3同，只是左右方向相反。

【意念】

與「向右平帶」動作3同。

(3) Bow Step and Withdraw Sword to Left

Hold the sword with the blade flat. Turn the right hand over and draw the sword to the left back in an arc in front of the left ribs, force on the edge. The left sword finger continues to move up in an arc to the left side over the head, palm facing diagonally up. Shift the weight forward. Bend the left leg forward to form a left Bow Step. Eyes look at the tip of the sword (Figure 3-18).

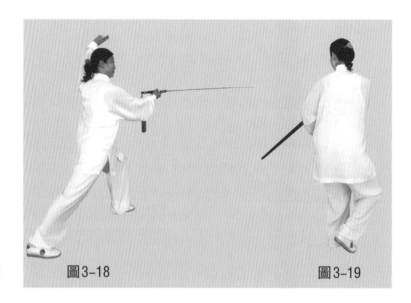

圖3-18　　　　　圖3-19

Key Points

Excluding the left Sword Fingers, which draw an arc upward, the rest of the movement is the same as "Bow Step and Withdraw Sword to Right" in the opposite direction.

Keep in Mind

See "Keep in Mind" for "Bow step and Withdraw Sword to Right".

六、獨立掄劈（哪吒探海）

1. 轉體掄劍

上體左轉，右腳收至左腳內側，腳尖點地。右手持劍由前向下向後畫弧，立劍置於上體左下方；左劍指下落於右肩前，兩臂在體前交叉，眼向後看（圖3-19）。

【要領】

（1）右手持劍後掄時手心斜向外；左手劍指，手心斜向前下。

（2）上體左轉要保持正直，不要前俯。上體左轉幅度要大，面向西北為宜。

【意念】

（1）注意肩鬆沉，以腰帶動劍下按。

（2）提右腳，吸氣縮右胯，周身氣沉，鬆靜地完成動作。

6. Swing and Chop with One Leg Standing

(Nézhā Explores the Sea)

(1) Turn Body and Swing Sword

Turn the upper body to the left and place the right foot beside the left foot, only the toes touching the ground. The right hand wields the sword first downward, then backward to draw an arc and erects the sword at the lower left side of the upper body. The left Sword Fingers stop in front of the left shoulder. The two arms are crossed in front of body. Eyes look ahead (Figure 3-19).

Key Points

(1) When swinging the sword backward, the right palm faces diagonally outward; the left palm faces diagonally down.

(2) Keep the upper body upright while turning left. Don't bend forward. The upper body turns left to face the northwest.

Keep in Mind

(1) Relax and sink shoulders. The waist leads the sword to be pressed down.

(2) Lift the right foot; pull the right hip in; inhale. The entire body is full of the energy; complete the movement relaxingly and peacefully.

2. 上步舉劍

右腳向前上步，腳跟著地。同時，右手持劍內旋上舉於頭上方，左手劍指翻轉，手心向上，收於腰部，頭轉向前方，眼向前看（圖3-20a、圖3-20b）。

【要領】

上步、舉劍、轉腰、旋臂、轉頭應協調一致，同時完成。

【意念】

連接上動不停，鬆左腰腎，吸氣配合上體左轉帶動劍向上掄舉，頭要上領。

（2）Step Forward and Lift Sword

The right foot steps forward, only the heel touching the

圖3-20a　　　　圖3-20b

ground. Meanwhile, the right hand turns inward and lifts the sword above the head; the left Sword Fingers turn over and draw back to the waist, palm facing up. The head turns to the front. Eyes look ahead (Figure 3-20a, Figure 3-20b).

Key Points

Stepping forward, lifting the sword, turning the waist, rotating the arm, and turning the head are all coordinated with each other and finished at the same time.

Keep in Mind

Connect to the last movement without pause. Relax the waist on the left side. With inhaling coordinating, the upper body turns left and leads the sword swung up. Draw the head up.

3. 獨立劈劍

重心移向右腿,右腳踏實;左腿屈膝上提,成右獨立步。同時,上體稍右轉,稍前傾,右手持劍隨上體右轉向前下方立劍劈下,力達劍刃,右臂與劍成一斜線;左手劍指向後向上畫弧至左上方,掌心斜向上,眼看下方(圖3-21a、圖3-21b)。

【要領】

(1)獨立步右腳微向裏扣,腳尖向東偏北30°。

(2)右手持劍沿身體左側掄立圓,順勢向前下方劈出,劍尖與膝同高,上體微前傾,力達劍身。左臂向後上方圓滿撐開。

（3）左劍指向後上方畫弧，右手持劍掄立圓劈出，兩手應上下、前後對稱，交叉畫立圓，動作要連貫，不可中斷。

【意念】

意念在鬆右胯，沉氣轉腰，力貫劍刃，劍由上而下，配合呼氣助力，用腰身帶動下劈。

(3) Stand on One Leg and Chop Sword

Shift the weight onto the right leg, and place the foot on the ground firmly. Bend the left leg and lift it up to form One Leg Stance. At the same time, the upper body turns to the right

圖3-21a

圖3-21b

and leans forwards slightly. The right hand also turns to the right and chops the sword towards the lower front, force on the edge. The right arm is aligned with the sword. Meanwhile, the left Sword Fingers move backward, then upward and draw an arc to the upper left, with the palm facing diagonally up. Eyes look down (Figure 3–21a, Figure 3–21b).

Key Points

(1) For the One Leg Stance, the right foot turns inward slightly, the toes pointing to the east and 30° northwards.

(2) The right hand holds the sword and draws a vertical ellipse along the left side of the body, then splits towards the lower front, with the tip at the level of the knee. The upper body leans forward slightly and the force reaches the blade of the sword. The left arm is arched to the upper back.

(3) When the left Sword Fingers draw an arc towards the upper back, the right hand holds the sword and splits downward in an arc. The two hands draw circles correspondingly. The movement should be fluid.

Keep in Mind

Relax the right hip. Let the energy sink while turning the waist. Deliver the force to the edge of the sword. Exhale to increase the power. The waist leads the sword to chop down.

七、退步回抽（懷中抱月）

1. 退步提劍

左腳向後落下，右手持劍外旋上提，手心向上（圖3-22）。

【要領】

左腳向後落下要先屈右膝，左腳盡力向後跨步落下。

【意念】

鬆右胯，屈右膝，往後落步要吸氣。

7. Step Back and Withdraw Sword（Embrace the Moon）

(1) Step Backward and Draw the Sword Back

Move the left foot backward. Turn the right hand outward

圖3-22

and lift the sword, palm facing up (Figure 3–22).

Key Points

Bend the right knee before placing the left foot on the ground. The left foot takes a big step backward.

Keep in Mind

Relax the right hip. Bend the right knee. Step back and inhale.

2. 虛步回抽

重心後移，右腳隨之撤半步，前腳掌著地，成右虛步。同時，右手持劍抽回，劍柄收於左肋旁，手心向內，立劍，劍尖斜向上，左手劍指落於劍柄上，眼看劍尖（圖3-23a、圖3-23b）。

【要領】

（1）抽劍時右手持劍外旋上提，使劍翻轉，下刃向上立劍由前向後上弧抽回，力點沿下刃滑動，不可走直線。

（2）左腳後落步幅要大，重心移動要充分，右腳回撤要輕靈，兩腳虛實分明，不可成丁步。

（3）定勢虛步抱劍，兩臂要撐圓，上體左轉，劍尖斜向右上方，同時頭向右扭轉看前方，兩肩鬆沉，劍柄與身體相距20公分。

【意念】

重心後移，襠走上弧，背向後倚，先吸後呼，收合蓄勁。

(2) Empty Step and Withdraw Sword

While shifting the weight backward, the right foot takes a half step back, the forefoot touching the ground to form a right Empty Step. At the same time, the right hand draws the sword back with the hilt beside the left ribs, palm facing inward. Hold the sword with the tip pointing diagonally up. Place the left Sword Fingers on the handle. Eyes look at the tip (Figure 3-23a, Figure 3-23b).

圖3-23a　　　　　圖3-23b

Key Points

(1) Lift the right hand and rotate it outward to turn over the sword, the lower edge up. Draw the sword, vertical, backward in an upward arc, force moving along the edge. Do not move in a straight line.

(2) The left foot takes a big step back. Shift the weight completely. Bring the right foot in lightly. The feet form the Empty Step distinctly. Do not form a T-step.

(3) At the posture to hold the sword in an Empty Step, both arms maintain arched. Turn the upper body to the left, the tip of the sword pointing to the upper right, and turn the head to the right to look ahead. Relax and sink the shoulders. The handle of the sword is about 20cm away from the body.

Keep in Mind

Shift the weight backward. Move the crotch in an upward arc. Draw the back backwards. Inhale first and then exhale to increase the power.

八、獨立上刺（宿鳥投林）

1. 轉體墊步

身體右轉，面向前方，右腳稍向前墊步，腳跟著地。同時，右手持劍轉至腹前，手心向上；左手劍指隨右手轉動仍附於右腕部，平劍、劍尖斜向上，眼看劍尖（圖3-24）。

【要領】

身體轉正，墊步幅度為半腳，動步要輕靈。

【意念】

氣沉，落胯，兩肩放鬆。

8. Thrust Upward with One Leg Standing

（Bird Returns to Tree at Dusk）

(1) Body Turns and Skip

Turn the body to the right to face the front. The right foot skips forward slightly, only the heel touching the ground. Meanwhile, the right hand holds the sword and moves in front of the abdomen, palm facing up. The left Sword Fingers stay on the wrist of the right hand and follow it moving. The blade of the

圖3-24

sword is flat with the tip pointing diagonally up. Eyes look at the tip of the sword (Figure 3–24).

Key Points

Turn the body to face the front. The right foot skips a half step forward. The step is light and quick.

Keep in Mind

Sink the energy; sink the hips. Relax the shoulders.

2. 提膝上刺

重心前移，右腳外撇，全腳踏實；左腿屈膝提起，成右獨立步。同時，右手持劍，左手附於右腕，向前上方刺出，右手心向上，平劍，力貫劍尖，劍尖略高於頭（圖3–25）。

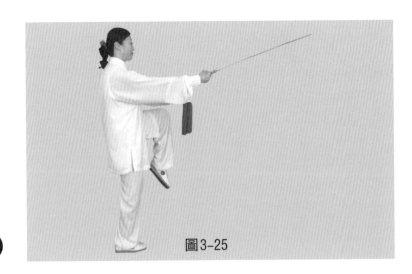

圖3-25

【要領】

（1）上刺時，手與肩同高，兩臂微屈，不可聳肩。

（2）左膝提起向正前，小腿與腳略向裏護襠，左腳面自然展平，腳尖向下。

【意念】

（1）身體中正，鬆右胯，頭要上領。

（2）百會與會陰上下對拉，呼氣配合，勁貫劍尖，神態自然。

（2）Lift Knee and Thrust up

Shift the weight forward. Turn the right foot outward, with the whole foot on the ground solidly. Bend the left leg and lift it up to form One Leg Stance. Meanwhile, thrust it to the upper front with the blade flat, palm facing up. The force is focused on the tip, which is a little higher than head level. The left hand is on the right wrist (Figure 3-25).

Key Points

（1）When thrusting up, the hand is at shoulder level. Both arms are bent slightly. Do not lift the shoulders.

（2）Lift the left knee to face the front, draw the lower leg and the foot in slightly to protect the crotch. The left foot is stretched naturally and the toes point down.

Keep in Mind

（1）Keep the body upright and right hip relaxed. Draw the

head up.

(2) Pull the "Bai Hui" and "Hui Yin" to the opposite directions ("Bai Hui" is an acupuncture point, which is at the centre of the top of the head. "Hui Yin" is an acupuncture point, which is at the centre of the crotch). Exhale in co-ordination. Deliver the force to the tip of the sword. Manners are natural.

第二組

九、虛步下截（烏龍擺尾）

1. 轉體擺劍

左腳向左後方落步，重心移至左腳，上體左轉。同時，右手持劍隨上體左轉向左平擺，手心向上；左手劍指翻轉下落挎於左腰間，手心向上，眼看劍尖（圖3-26）。

【要領】

（1）左腳向左後落步要輕緩，不可「砸夯」。

（2）向左轉體帶動右手持劍平擺，右臂自然舒展，高與肩平，劍尖指向右方。

（3）上體自然正直。

【意念】

吸氣，兩肩逆向順勁。

Group 2

9. Intercept Downward with Empty Step

（Black Dragon Whips Tail）

（1）Turn Body and Swing Sword

The left foot steps to the left back. Turn the upper body to the left. Shift the weight onto the left foot. Meanwhile, swing the sword horizontally to the left, palm facing up. Turn the left Sword Fingers over and move it down to the left side of the waist, palm facing up. Eyes look at the tip of the sword(Figure 3-26).

Key Points

（1）The left foot steps towards the left back lightly and slowly. Do not make a heavy step.

（2）Turn the body to the left and lead the right hand to

圖3-26

swing the sword with the blade flat. Extend the right arm naturally at shoulder level. The tip of the sword points right.

(3) Keep the upper body naturally upright.

Keep in Mind

Inhale and push the shoulders in the opposite directions of the sword.

2. 虛步下截

　　上體右轉，右腳輕輕提起向東北方向落下，腳尖點地，成右虛步。同時，右手持劍隨轉體旋臂翻腕，經體前向右向下截按，劍尖斜下垂，高與膝平；左手劍指向左向上弧形上繞舉於左上方，掌心斜向上，眼視右前方（圖3-27）。

圖3-27

【要領】

（1）下截劍時要以腰向右轉動帶動右臂向右下方截按，身、劍、手、腳、眼動作要協調一致，同時到位。右臂略屈，不可挺直，劍身置於身體右側與身體平行。

（2）右虛步要向東北30°，轉頭目視東南，右腳方向與視角方向夾角約90°。

（3）兩腳橫向距離為10公分，不可交叉或過寬。

【意念】

（1）注意腰部兩腎抽提，兩側腰肌「S」形扭轉，交替鬆沉，帶動劍下截。

（2）完成動作過程中先吸氣後呼氣，以助勁力貫於劍身前、中部位。

(2) Intercept Down in Empty Step

Turn the upper body to the right. Lift the right foot gently and place the toes on the ground to point north-east and form a right Empty Step. Meanwhile, the right arm follows the body and the right hand turns over to intercept to the lower right in front of the body. The tip of the sword is pointing diagonally down at knee level. The left Sword Fingers draw an arc to the upper left, palm facing up diagonally. Eyes look the right front (Figure 3-27).

Key Points

（1）When intercepting downward, turn the waist to the right, leading the right arm to cut down toward the lower right. The motions of the body, sword, hands, feet and eyes are co-ordinated with each other and finished at the same time. Bend the right arm slightly; do not be stiff. The blade of the sword is at the right side of the body and is parallel to the body.

（2）The Right Empty Step points 30° east of north. Eyes look to the south-east 90° from the direction of the right foot.

（3）The horizontal distance of the feet is about 10 cm; they should not be too wide or too close.

Keep in Mind

（1）Pull and raise the waist. Twist the muscles at the waist so that the body forms an S-shape. Alternate between relaxing and sinking the waist to lead the sword intercepting down.

（2）Inhale first and then exhale to deliver the force to the front and middle part of the sword.

十、左弓步刺（青龍出水）

1. 退步提劍

右手持劍向體前提起，高與胸平，劍尖指向左前下方，同時，左手劍指下落於右腕部。右腳提起向側後撤步，腳尖著地，眼看劍尖（圖3-28）。

【要領】

（1）右手持劍是上提，不可前刺。

（2）右腿隨劍上提先屈膝提起，再向側後伸出撤退步，撤退方向在正南偏西30°。

【意念】

左腳下踩，鬆右胯，提膝、提劍一致，前送劍、後退步一致，似一線向兩端延伸，配合吸氣，全身鬆沉。

10. Thrust in Left Bow Step

（Green Dragon Emerges from Water）

（1）Step Back and Lift Sword

Raise the sword in front of the body at chest level, the tip pointing to the lower left front. At the same time, place the left Sword Fingers on the wrist of the right hand. The right foot

圖3-28

steps to the right back, only the toes touching the ground. Eyes look at the tip of the sword (Figure 3–28).

Key Points

(1) Lift the sword only; do not thrust it forward.

(2) Following the sword, bend the right leg and move it backward to 30° west of south.

Keep in Mind

The step with the left foot is coordinated with the relaxing left hip and the lifting knee and sword. The sword moving forward is coordinated with the foot stepping back; push them in the opposite directions. Relax and sink the entire body, inhaling.

2. 轉體撤劍

重心向右腿移動，上體右轉。同時，右手持劍隨轉體經面前向右側後抽撤，手心翻轉向下；左手劍指仍附於右腕，隨劍一同後撤，眼看右手（圖3–29）。

【要領】

（1）右手持劍回撤，前臂內旋，手心向下，由拇指與中指、無名指控制劍柄，劍尖不可擺動，平劍撤抽。

（2）上體保持正直，不可前俯、右歪，襠走下弧。

【意念】

撤劍要鬆肩、垂肘，節節抽撤，吸氣下沉。

(2) Turn Body and Withdraw Sword

Shift the weight onto the right leg. Turn the body to the right. Meanwhile, the right hand passes in front of the head, draws the sword to the right back, and turns the palm to face down. The left Sword Fingers are still resting on the right wrist and follow the sword back. Eyes look at the right hand (Figure 3–29).

Key Points

(1) Rotate the right forearm inward, palm facing down. The right hand draws the sword back, which is controlled by the thumb, middle finger and third finger. Do not swing the tip of the sword. Withdraw the sword with blade flat.

(2) Keep the upper body upright; do not bend it forward or backward. Move the crotch in a downward arc.

圖3-29

Keep in Mind

Relax the shoulders and sink the elbows while withdrawing the sword successively. Inhale and sink the energy（Qi）.

3. 收腳收劍

上體左轉，左腳收至右腳內側。右手持劍隨轉體向下捲收於右腰側，左劍指亦隨之翻轉收至腹前，眼由右向左前方看（圖3-30）。

【要領】

劍尖方向始終對著左前方，既不外擺，也不可下垂。持劍前臂外旋有捲動之意。

【意念】

意氣下沉，鬆肩垂肘。捲腕收劍要吸氣。

（3）Bring in Foot and Withdraw Sword

Turn the upper body to the left. Place the left foot beside the right foot. Following the body, the right hand holds the sword and draws back to the right side of the waist. The left Sword Fingers accordingly turn over and move in the front of the abdomen. Eyes look at the left front（Figure 3-30）.

Key Points

Keep the tip of the Sword to point to the left front; do not swing it outward or point down. Turn the forearm outward with the intention to rotate it.

Keep in Mind

Sink the energy. Relax the shoulders and sink the elbows. Inhale while turning the wrist and withdrawing the sword.

4. 弓步平刺

　　左腳向左前邁出，腳跟著地，重心前移，左腿屈膝前弓，全腳著地，成左弓步。同時，上體左轉，右手持劍從右腰間向左前方平劍刺出，高與胸平，手心向上，力達劍尖；左劍指向左向上繞至左上方，手心斜向上，臂圓撐，眼看劍尖（圖3-31）。

　　【要領】

　　（1）左弓步方向為左前方（東北方向30°～45°），

圖3-30　　　　　圖3-31

弓步時邁步應輕靈，不可「砸夯」，上體正直，鬆腰鬆胯。

（2）刺劍時為平劍，臂與劍一條直線，高與胸平。

（3）劍的回撤、下捲、刺出都要以腰帶動完成。劍尖不可擺動，動作要連貫，自然圓潤。

【意念】

沉氣、落胯，弓步襠走下弧，勁起腳下氣貼背，傳於劍，刺劍呼氣助力。

(4) Bow Step and Thrust Sword

The left foot steps towards the left front, only the heel touching the ground. Shift the weight forward. Bend the left leg and place the entire foot on the ground to form a left Bow Step. At the same time, turn the upper body to the left. The right hand holds the sword with the blade flat and thrusts from the right side of the waist to the front left, at chest level, palm facing up and force on the tip. The left Sword Fingers move to the upper left, palm facing up diagonally, the arm arched. Eyes look at the tip of the sword (Figure 3–31).

Key Points

（1）The left Bow Step points to the front left (about the direction of north east). Steps lightly; avoid a heavy step. Keep the upper body upright and the waist and hips relaxed.

（2）The sword is thrust with the blade flat and kept aligned with the arm at chest level.

（3）The waist leads to withdraw, rotate and thrust the sword; do not swing the tip from one side to another. The movement should be continuous, natural and fluent.

Keep in Mind

Sink the energy（Qi）and sink the hips. Move the crotch in a downward arc. The force is generated from the foot, delivered to the sword and increased by exhaling.

十一、轉身斜帶（風捲荷葉）

1. 扣腳收劍

重心後移，左腳尖裏扣，上體右轉。同時，右手持劍屈臂微收，手心向上，左劍指下落於右腕部，眼看劍尖（圖3-32）。

【要領】

左腳尖儘量裏扣，兩肩要鬆沉，上體後倚保持正直。

【意念】

注意右膝、右胯鬆沉，上體後坐要背倚，吸氣下沉。

11. Turn Body and Withdraw Sword Diagonally

（Wind Blows Lotus Leaves）

(1) Turn Foot inward and Withdraw Sword

Shifting the weight backward, swing the left toes inward. Turn the upper body to the right. Meanwhile, bend the right arm slightly to draw back the sword, palm facing up. Place the left Sword Fingers on the right wrist. Eyes look at the tip of the sword (Figure 3-32).

Key Points

Swing the left toes inward as much as possible. Relax and sink the shoulders. The upper body leans back slightly.

Keep in Mind

Relax and sink the right knee and hip. Shift the weight backward. The upper body leans back. Sink the energy (Qi) and inhale.

2. 收腳轉體

上體右轉，重心移至左腿，左腿屈膝半蹲；右腳提起，收貼於左小腿內側。右手持劍繼續後收於胸腰之間，手心向上，左劍指仍附於右腕，眼看劍尖（圖3-33）。

【要領】

收腳時，左腿屈膝半蹲，不可成獨立步。

【意念】

意注左胯，心靜體鬆，深吸氣。

(2) Withdraw foot and turn body

While the upper body turns to the right, shift the weight onto the left leg and bend the leg to a half squat. Lift the right foot and place it beside the left lower leg. The right hand holds the sword and places between the chest and waist, palm facing up. The left Sword Fingers are still on the right wrist. Eyes look at the tip of the sword (Figure 3–33).

Key Points

When bringing the left foot in, bend the left leg to a half squat. Do not form a One Leg Stand.

圖3-32

圖3-33

Keep in Mind

Focus on the left hip. Keep the mind peaceful and the body relaxed. Breathe deeply.

3. 弓步右帶

左腿微微屈膝下蹲，右腳向右前邁出，腳跟先著地，再屈膝前弓，全腳踏實，成右弓步。同時，右手持劍向左前送出，並隨上體右轉，翻腕，手心向下，弧線向右平帶，力在右手小指一側劍刃，左劍指仍附於右腕部，眼看劍尖（圖3-34）。

【要領】

（1）弓步方向為正西偏北30°，從上動左弓步到本動右弓步轉體在250°左右。

圖3-34

（2）斜帶劍只是說劍勢走向，要領與「平帶劍」一樣。劍尖可略高，劍走勢為半橢圓形。

【意念】

動作運轉似磨盤轉動，以腰為軸，帶劍運轉，身劍相合，呼氣配合。

(3) Withdraw Sword in right Bow Step

Bend the left leg slightly into a half squat. The right leg steps to the right front and place the heel on the ground first, then bend the knee forward, placing the entire foot on the ground solidly to form a right Bow Step. At the same time, the right hand pushes the sword towards the left front and the body turns to the right. The wrist is turned over and the palm is facing down to withdraw the sword to the right with a flat blade. The force is on the edge on the same side of the little finger. The left Sword Fingers stay on the right wrist. Eyes look at the tip of the sword (Figure 3–34).

Key Points

（1）The Bow Step 30° north of west. The body turns about 250° from the left Bow Step of the last movement to the right Bow Step.

（2）The rest of the Key Points are the same as "withdraw sword with blade Flat", please refer to movement 4, "Withdraw Sword to the Right (Block and Sweep to the Right)". The only difference is the direction is diagonally. The tip of the sword is slightly higher than the blade. Move the sword in an arc.

Keep in Mind

Move as if using a stone grinder. The waist acts as the axle to lead the sword to swing. The body and sword unite as one, accompanied by exhaling.

十二、縮身斜帶（獅子搖頭）

1. 收腳收劍

左腳收至右腳內側，同時，右手持劍收於右腰側，左手劍指停於右腕部，眼看前方（圖3-35）。

【要領】

上體保持正直，稍向右轉。

【意念】

意注右胯，沉歸丹田，手腳相合，配以深吸氣。

12. Retreat and Withdraw Sword

(Lion Shakes its Mane)

(1) Bring Foot in and Withdraw Sword

Place the left foot beside of the right foot. Meanwhile, the right hand draws back the sword to the right side of the waist. Place the left Sword Fingers on the right wrist. Eyes look at the front (Figure 3–35).

Key Points

Keep the upper body upright and turn it to the right slightly.

Keep in Mind

Focus on the right hip. Sink the energy (Qi) to the abdomen. Hands and feet are co-ordinated; breathe deeply.

2. 撤步送劍

左腳撤步落於原位，右手持劍走外弧前送，左劍指屈肘經左肋反插，向身後穿出，手心向後，眼看前方（圖3-36）。

【要領】

前送劍要前探，上體略前傾。送劍方向與弓步方

圖3-36

圖3-35

向一致。

【意念】

意注丹田，向四肢擴散。襠部要圓。劍與劍指要前後對拉。呼氣沉胯。

(2) Step Back and Send out Sword

The left foot falls to the original position. While the right hand moves in an arc to send out the sword, the left Sword Fingers move along the ribs to the back of the body by bending the arm, palm facing back. Eyes look at the front (Figure 3-36).

Key Points

The upper body leans forward slightly when sending out the sword. The sword points in the same direction as the Bow Step.

Keep in Mind

Focus on abdomen and the limbs. The crotch is rounded. Push the sword and the Sword Fingers away from each other. Sink the hips and exhale.

3. 丁步帶劍

重心向左腿移動，右腳收至左腳內側點地成丁步。同時，右手持劍翻轉，手心向上，將劍向左平帶，力點在劍刃滑動，左劍指向上向前弧形落於右腕部，眼看劍尖（圖3-37）。

【要領】

收腳帶劍時上體左轉，重心穩穩落於左腿，上體保持正直，頭上頂，鬆腰胯，臀部不可外凸，上體不可前俯。

【意念】

意想上體左轉時落胯沉氣，以腰平穩回帶劍身。

(3) T-shape Step and Withdraw Sword

Shift the weight to the left leg. Place the right foot beside the left foot to form T-shape Step. At the same time, the right hand turns over, palm facing up, and draws the sword to the left with the blade flat, force moving along the edge of the sword. The left Sword Fingers move in an arc down to the wrist of the right hand. Eyes look at the tip of the sword (Figure

圖3-37

3-37）.

Key Points

While bringing the foot back and withdrawing the sword, turn the upper body to the left and shift the weight onto the left leg. Keep the upper body upright. Draw the head up. Relax the waist and hips. Do not push the buttocks out. Do not bend the upper body forward.

Keep in Mind

When the upper body turns left, sink the hip and the energy. The waist leads to draw back the sword.

十三、提膝捧劍（虎抱頭）

1. 虛步分手

右腳後退一步，重心後移；左腳微動，腳尖著地成左虛步。同時，兩手前送，再向上體兩側分開，手心均向下，劍尖裏斜，劍身置於上體右側，劍尖向前，眼看前方（圖3-38）。

【要領】

（1）兩手分開，兩臂圓撐，兩手高與腰平，劍尖裏斜於體前中線附近，不可外撇。

（2）右腳後撇步時，腰先右轉，兩手分開將到位時再將上體左轉面向前方。右轉、左轉幅度不宜過大，與兩臂分展協調配合。

【意念】

（1）右腳後撤時，氣注左腳，重心平穩。

（2）兩臂左右分開時氣注右腳，呼氣沉胯，肩要鬆沉，肘要墜，兩手有下按感。

13. Lift Knee and Hold Sword with Both Hands

（Tiger Holds its Head）

（1）Separate Hands in Empty Step

The right foot steps backward and shift the weight backward. The left foot moves slightly, only the toes touching the ground to form a left Empty Step. Meanwhile, move both hands forward first, and then separate them to the sides respectively, palms facing down, and the tip of the sword pointing inwards obliquely. The sword stops at the right side of the body, the tip

圖3-38

pointing forward. Eyes look at the front (Figure 3–38).

Key Points

（1）While the hands are separated, the arms are arched, hands at the waist level. The tip of the sword tilts inward to the centre of the body.

（2）While the right foot steps backward, turn the waist to the right first. When the hands move to the sides of the body, turn the upper body to the left to face the front. The waist should not turn right or left too much and it should be coordinated with the arms.

Keep in Mind

（1）When the right foot steps back, sink the energy（Qi） to the left foot and keep the weight stable.

（2）When separating the arms, sink the energy（Qi）to the right foot. Exhale and sink the hip. Sink the shoulders and elbows. The hands should feel as if being pressed down.

2. 提膝捧劍

左腳略向前墊步，重心移於左腿；右腿提膝於體前，成左獨立步。同時，兩手向前合抱於胸前，右手持劍將手翻轉，手心向上，左手劍指變掌捧托於右手背下方，兩臂屈圓，劍身平置體前，劍尖向前，目視前方（圖3–39）。

【要領】

（1）兩手合抱時身體下沉，兩手先微向下向外再向前在胸前相合捧劍。

（2）提右腿時左膝微屈，右腿向前弧形擺至體前再屈小腿，成獨立步。

（3）完成全部動作要勻緩，柔和。

【意念】

（1）意注左腳，氣沉丹田，提膝上步，沉肩垂肘，鬆腰鬆胯。

（2）兩手合抱，氣貼脊背，吸氣，經兩臂傳送合勁於劍，頭上頂。

（2）Lift Knee and Hold Sword with Both Hands

Move the left foot forward slightly, and shift the weight onto

圖3-39

the left leg. Lift the right leg and form a Left One Leg Stand. Meanwhile, hold both hands together in front of the chest. The right hand holds the sword and turns over. The left hand holds the right hand on its back, palms facing up and arms rounded. The blade of the sword is flat in front of the body, tip pointing forward. Eyes look at the front (Figure 3–39).

Key Points

(1) When holding the hands together, move the hands downward and outward first and then forward to hold the sword in front of chest.

(2) When lifting the right leg, bend the left knee slightly. Move the right leg in an arc in front of the body first, and then bend the lower leg to form One Leg Stand.

(3) Complete the movement evenly and gently.

Keep in Mind

(1) Focus on the left foot. Sink the energy (Qi) to the abdomen. Lift the knee to step forward. Sink the shoulders and elbows. Relax the waist and hips.

(2) While two hands are joined together, deliver the energy (Qi) along the spine; inhaling; deliver the force to the sword. Draw the head up.

十四、跳步平刺（野馬跳澗）

1. 落腳送劍

右腳前落，腳跟著地。兩手捧劍向下向裏，弧線向上至胸前再向前送劍，眼看前方（圖3-40）。

【要領】

（1）右腳落地時上體保持垂直升降，步幅不宜過大，上體不可前俯。

（2）兩手合抱畫圓與身體升降要協調配合。

【意念】

（1）完成動作意氣下沉，全身之氣向丹田歸聚。

（2）送劍時，吸氣配合沉肩墜肘，兩手與脊背微微對撐。

圖3-40

14. Hop and Thrust Sword with Blade Flat

（Wild Horse Leaps Over Creek）

(1) Place the Foot Down and Send Out the Sword

The right foot steps forward with only the heel touching the ground. Both hands hold the sword and move downward then backward in front of the chest and thrust it forward. Eyes look at the front (Figure 3–40).

Key Points

（1）When placing the right foot down on the ground, move the upper body up and down vertically; do not bend forward; do not make a big step.

（2）The motions of drawing an arc with the hands should co-ordinate with the body moving up and down.

Keep in Mind

（1）Sink and collect the energy（Qi）from all over the body to abdomen.

（2）When moving the sword forward, sink the shoulders and elbows; inhale. Push the hands and the back in opposite directions.

2. 捧劍前刺

重心前移至右腿，蹬地送髖，頭頂，左腳離地，左腿自然後伸。同時，兩手捧劍向前伸刺，眼看前方

（圖3-41）。

【要領】

劍前伸刺時，高度與胸平，兩臂要舒展，百會穴上領。左腿自然伸直，左腳面展平。

【意念】

（1）右腳踩實，氣起腳底，提氣貼背，貫頂，勁達劍尖，呼氣助力。

（2）劍向前伸刺，左腳後擺，對稱平衡。

(2) Hold Sword and Thrust with Both Hands

Shift the weight onto the right leg. Push the ground and lift the left hip backward. Draw the head up. Lift the left foot off the ground and extend the leg backward naturally. At the same time, both hands hold the sword and thrust forward. Eyes look

圖3-41

at the front (Figure 3-41).

Key Points

When thrusting the sword forward, keep it at chest level; the arms are stretched but remain comfortable. Draw the "Bai Hui" up ("Bai Hui" is an acupuncture point, which is at the centre of the top of the head). The left leg and the left foot are stretched naturally.

Keep in Mind

(1) Place the right foot on the ground solidly. The energy (Qi) is raised from the sole of the foot, along the back, and to the top of the head. Deliver the force to the tip of the sword; exhale to increase its power.

(2) When thrusting the sword forward, swing the left leg backward to obtain balance.

3. 跳步分劍

右腳蹬地，左腳隨即前跨一步踏實，右腳在左腳將落地時迅速提起向左小腿內側收攏。同時，兩手分撤至胯兩側，手心均向下，左手變為劍指，眼看前方（圖3-42）。

【要領】

（1）向前跳步不要過高，動作要輕靈柔和，不可做成走步。

（2）左腳落地時腳微外撇，膝關節彎曲緩衝，重心穩定在左腳。

（3）兩手分撒時兩手直線收至兩胯側，兩臂不可外擺。

【意念】

跳步時要提氣，頭上領，上體拔背而出，不要前俯。落地時呼氣，收右腳時轉為吸氣。

(3) Jump and Separate Hands

The right foot pushes the ground forcefully. The left foot takes a jump forward and falls on the ground firmly. Raise the right foot quickly to the inside of the left lower leg just before the left foot falls on the ground. In the meantime, separate the hands to the sides of the hips, palms facing down. Turn the left

圖3-42

hand into Sword Fingers. Eyes look at the front（Figure 3–42）.

Key Points

（1）Do not jump too high, but make sure both feet are off the ground. The motion should be light and gentle.

（2）When placing the left foot on the ground, swing it outward slightly. Bend the knee. The weight is on the left foot.

（3）The hands move in a line to the sides of the hips. Do not swing the arms outward.

Keep in Mind

When jumping forward, raise the energy（Qi）up; draw the head and back up; do not bend forward. Exhale when the foot is falling on the ground; inhale when bringing the right foot back.

4. 弓步平刺

右腳向前上步，屈膝前弓，重心前移成右弓步。同時，右手持劍向前平刺，手心向上，劍與臂成直線；同時左手劍指繞舉至額頭左上方，手心斜向外，目視劍尖（圖3–43）。

【要領】

鬆腰順肩，不可扭腰歪胯。弓步時兩腳不可踩在一條直線上，亦不可交叉成麻花步。

【意念】

（1）弓步平刺注意鬆腰、圓襠，走下弧。

（2）上體保持中正，刺劍與劍指要兩頭對撐，力透脊背，勁貫劍尖，呼氣助力。

(4) Bow Step and Thrust Sword with Blade Flat

Move the right foot forward and bend the knee. Shift the weight forward to form the right Bow Step. Meanwhile, thrust the sword forward with the blade flat, the palm facing up and the sword on one line with the arm. Move the left Sword Fingers up to the left upside of the forehead, palm facing outward diagonally. Eyes look at the tip of the sword (Figure 3–43).

Key Points

Relax the waist and push the shoulder forward; do not twist the waist or lean the hip. The feet are in Bow Step; do not stand on the same line. The legs should not be crossed.

圖3-43

Keep in Mind

(1) To make the Bow Step, relax the waist; round the crotch and move it in a downward arc.

(2) Keep the upper body upright. Push the sword and the Sword Figures in opposite directions. Deliver the force through the back to the tip of the sword; exhale to increase the power.

十五、左虛步撩（小魁星）

1. 收腳繞劍

重心後移，上體左轉，右腳收至左腳前（腳尖可點地）。同時，右手持劍隨轉體向上向後畫弧，劍柄落於左腰側，劍尖向上，左劍指落於右腕部，眼向左看（圖3-44）。

圖3-44

【要領】

（1）劍向後繞時上體轉動幅度要大，眼神隨劍轉視。繞劍要貼近身體，劍尖不可擺動。

（2）右臂要先外旋後內旋，將手心轉向裏側。

【意念】

收右腳時注意左胯、左膝、左踝依次放鬆，背部向後依，全身勁內收，勁貫劍身，吸氣助勁。

15. Slice Sword Upward with Left Empty Stance

（The Little Dipper）

(1) Bring in Foot and Swing Sword

Shift the weight backward. Turn the upper body to the left. Place the right foot before the left foot（the toes can touch the ground）. Meanwhile, following the body, the right hand moves the sword to the upper back, drawing an arc. The handle of the sword falls at the left side of the waist, tip pointing up. Place the left Sword Fingers on the wrist of the right hand. Eyes look to the left（Figure 3–44）.

Key Points

（1）When swinging the sword backward, the upper body makes a big tune. Eyes follow the sword. Place the sword close to the body; do not sway the tip.

（2）Rotate the right arm outward first and then inward, leading the palm to face inward.

When bringing the right foot in, relax the left hip, the left knee and the left ankle orderly. The back leans backward. Gather the energy from the whole body and deliver the force to the sword; assist by inhaling.

2. 墊步繞劍

上體稍右轉，右腳向前墊步，腳跟著地，腳尖外撇。同時，右手持劍隨轉體向下繞至體前，劍斜置於身體左側；左手劍指仍附於右腕，眼看前方（圖3-45）。

【要領】

劍要貼身繞動，劍尖指向後下方，不可觸地。

【意念】

氣注右腳，落胯上步，慢呼氣。

(2) Skip and Swing Sword

Turn the upper body right slightly. The right foot skips (Dian Bu) forward, only the heel touching the ground and the toes turning outward. Meanwhile, the right hand moves the sword in an arc downward and stops in front of body, with the sword slanted at the left side of the body. The left Sword Fingers are still on the wrist of the right hand. Eyes look at the front (Figure 3-45).

Key Points

The sword should be swung close to the body. The tip point to the lower back ; avoid touching the ground.

Keep in Mind

Sink the energy(Qi) to the right foot. Sink the hip to step forward. Exhale slowly.

3. 虛步左撩

　　上體繼續右轉，右腳踏實，重心移至右腿；左腳隨即進步，腳尖著地，成左虛步。同時，右手持劍，同附在右腕的劍指一起隨轉體上步向前撩出，停於右額前上方，右手心向外，劍尖斜向下，眼看前方（圖3-46）。

圖3-45　　　　　　　圖3-46

【要領】

（1）本式為左撩劍，要領是一要貼身，二要走立圓，臂要內旋，定勢右手心向外，活把握劍，虎口朝下，無名指、小指吃力，勁貫劍中前端。

（2）劍的繞行要在腰的旋轉下帶動完成，連貫圓潤，不可做成攔劍動作。

【意念】

意想右胯放鬆，氣下沉，上體右轉，意注劍刃，呼氣配合，劍由下向上撩出。

(3) Empty Step and Slice Sword Upward on Left

Continue to turn the upper body to the right. Place the right foot on the ground solidly and shift the weight onto the right leg. The left foot steps forward, the toes touching the ground to form a left Empty Step. At the same time, the right hand, with the left Sword Fingers still on the wrist, holds the sword to slice upward. Stop it above the right side of the forehead, the right palm facing outward. The tip of the sword points obliquely downward. Eyes look at the front (Figure 3-46).

Key Points

（1）This movement is Left Upward Slice. The sword should move in a vertical ellipse close to the body. Rotate the right arm inward. When it is settled, hold the sword loosely; palm is facing outward and the "Tiger Mouth" facing downward.

（ "Tiger Mouth" is where the thumb and index finger are joined）The sword is mainly controlled by the third finger and little finger. Deliver the force to the middle and front part of the sword.

（2）The swinging of the sword should be led by the waist, and keep continuous and smooth. Do not confuse it with the Parry Sword（Lan Jian）.

Keep in Mind

Relax the right hip and sink the energy（Qi）. Focus on the edge of the sword while turning the upper body to the right. Co-ordinated by exhaling, the sword is sliced upward.

十六、右弓步撩（水中撈月）

1. 轉體繞劍

身體右轉，同時右手持劍向後向下畫圓回繞，劍身豎立於上體右後側，手心向外，虎口朝上，左劍指隨劍繞行於右肩前，眼看劍尖（圖3-47）。

【要領】

劍向後畫圓回繞，眼要隨劍轉視，上體較大幅向右轉體。

【意念】

鬆肩、落臂，吸氣沉胯。

16. Slice Sword Upward with Right Bow Step

（Scoop the Moon from Bottom of Sea）

(1) Turn Body and Swing Sword

Turn the body to the right. The right hand moves the sword backward and downward to draw an arc until the sword erects behind the right side of the upper body. At this point, the palm faces outward and the "tiger mouth" faces up. The left Sword Fingers, following the sword, move in front of the right shoulder. Eyes look at the tip of the sword （Figure 3–47）.

Key Points

When moving the sword in an arc, the eyes follow the sword. The upper body makes a big tune to the right.

Keep in Mind

Relax the shoulders；sink the arms；sink the hips while inhaling.

2. 墊步繞劍

上體微左轉，重心下沉，左腳向前墊步，腳尖外撇。同時，右手持劍微向下繞，劍柄落於右胯旁，手心向外，劍尖朝後，左劍指畫弧至右腹前，手心向上，眼隨劍視（圖3-48）。

【要領】

持劍要活，劍尖不可觸地。

【意念】

全身向下鬆沉，開襠上步，身催步走，全身勁合。

(2) Skip and Swing Sword

Turn the upper body to the left slightly. Lower the weight. The left foot skips forward, the toes turning outward. Meanwhile, the right hand moves the sword downward slightly, the handle of the sword at the side of the right hip, palm facing outward and the tip of the sword pointing backward. The left Sword Fingers draw an arc to the right front of the abdomen, the palm facing up. Eyes follow the sword (Figure 3–48).

Key Points

Hold the sword flexibly and avoid the tip of the sword touching the ground.

圖3-47　　　圖3-48

Keep in Mind

Relax and sink the entire body downward. Open the crotch while stepping forward. The body leads the step. Gather the energy from the whole body.

3. 弓步撩劍

上體左轉不停，重心移至左腿，右腳向前進步，屈膝前弓，左腿自然伸直，成右弓步。同時，右手持劍由下向前反手立劍撩出，臂外旋，手心向外，高與肩平，劍尖略低；左劍指畫弧繞至左額上方，手心斜向上，眼看前方（圖3-49）。

【要領】

（1）右手持劍前撩時，右肩放鬆趁勢前順。

圖3-49

（2）弓步與前撩協調一致，同時到位。弓步兩腳橫向距離為10～20公分，兩腳不可成一線或交叉。

【意念】

氣向下沉，劍與右腿相隨而動，呼氣助勁，勁達劍中前部。

(3) Bow Step and Slice Sword Upward

Continue to turn the upper body to the left. Shift the weight onto the left leg. The right foot takes a step forward, the knee bent and the left leg stretched naturally to form right Bow Step. Meanwhile, turn the right arm outward. Slice with the sword to the upper front, the edge up, palm facing outward at shoulder level. The tip of the sword is slightly lower the blade. The left Sword Fingers draw an arc above the left side of the forehead, palm facing diagonally up. Eyes look ahead (Figure 3–49).

Key Points

（1）When the sword is sliced upward, relax the right shoulder and push it forward.

（2）The Bow Step should co-ordinate with the slicing and finish at the same time. The horizontal distance between the feet should be 10–20cm. The feet shouldn't be aligned or crossed.

Keep in Mind

Sink the energy (Qi) downward. The sword and right leg

follow each other. Deliver the force to the front part of the sword, assisted by exhaling.

第三組

十七、轉身回抽（射雁式）

1. 轉體收劍

身體左轉，重心後移，右腳腳尖裏扣，左腿屈膝，右腿蹬直成左側弓步。同時，右臂屈肘將劍收到體前，左劍指落於右腕，高與肩平，劍身平直，劍尖向後，眼看劍尖（圖3-50）。

【要領】

（1）轉體，重心左移時，右腳尖儘量裏扣，可

圖3-50

大於90°，成左側弓步。

（2）右臂屈肘收劍時用拇指、食指和虎口著力把握劍，其餘三指輔助鬆握。劍身要平直，眼回頭看劍尖。

【意念】

意念鬆右胯，屈肘。收劍時要吸氣，右肩向右胯沉勁。

Group 3

17. Turn Around and Withdraw Sword

（Shooting Wild Goose）

（1）Turn Around Body and Withdraw Sword

Turn the body to the left. Shift the weight backward. Swing the right toes inward. Bend the left leg and extend the right leg to form a left Side Bow Step. At the meantime, bend the right arm to withdraw the sword in front of body. Put the left Sword Fingers on the right wrist, at shoulder level. The blade of the sword is flat and straight, tip pointing to the back. Eyes look at the tip of the sword（Figure 3–50）.

Key Points

（1）While turning the body and shifting the weight to the left, turn the right toes inward as much as possible, more than 90° to form a left Side Bow Step.

（2）When bending the right arm to withdraw the sword,

control the sword with the thumb, the index finger and "tiger mouth"; the other three fingers grip loosely. The sword is flat and straight. Turn the head back to look at the tip of the sword.

Keep in Mind

Concentrate the mind to relax the right hip and bend the elbow. Inhale when withdrawing the sword, and sink the force from the right shoulder to the right hip.

2. 弓步劈劍

上體左轉不停，左腳尖稍外撇。同時，右手持劍向左前方劈下，眼看劍尖（圖3–51）。

【要領】

（1）本動要與上動連貫協調，不可斷動、斷勁。

（2）劈劍方向在東南（即中線偏右30°～45°），臂與劍平直。

【意念】

意想腰部回環，將勁貫於劍刃劈出，以呼氣助力。

(2) Chop in Bow Step

Continue to turn the upper body to the left. Swing the left toes slightly outward. Meanwhile, hold the sword and chop down to the left front. Eyes look at the tip of the sword (Figure 3–51).

Key Points

（1）This movement continues the last one; avoid interruption in both the moving and the energy.

（2）Chop sword toward the southeast（30° – 40° to the right of the centre of the body）. The sword aligns with the right arm.

Keep in Mind

Focus on the waist. Deliver the force to the edge of the sword and chop down. Exhale to increase the power.

3. 後坐抽劍

右腿屈膝，重心移至右腿。同時，右手持劍抽拉至右胯側，左劍指隨右腕後收，眼看右下方（圖3-52）。

圖3-51

圖3-52

【要領】

後坐抽劍時上體右轉，保持正直，不要凸臀。

【意念】

與上動連接不斷，腰再走回環，配合吸氣，以帶動劍的回抽。

(3) Sit Back and Pull Sword

Bend the right knee. Shift the weight to the right leg. The right hand brings the sword back to the side of the right hip. The left Sword Fingers follow the right wrist and draw backward too. Eyes look to the lower right (Figure 3–52).

Key Points

When shifting the weight backward and pulling the sword back, turn the upper body to the right and keep it upright. Don't push out the buttocks.

Keep in Mind

Connect to the last movement without interruption. Turn the waist to lead the sword back.

4. 虛步前指

上體繼續右轉再向左轉，左腳後撤半步，重心落至右腳，成左虛步。同時，右手持劍，隨腰右轉向右胯後抽劍，劍身斜置於身體右側，劍尖略低，左劍指向後向上經胸前下頜畫弧向前指出，高與眼平，眼看劍指（圖3–53）。

【要領】

（1）劍指前指、左腳點地、上體向左回轉要協調一致，同時完成，不可分割。

（2）虛步方向、劍指方向均向東偏南30°～40°。

（3）抽劍時要立劍走下弧回抽，力點在下劍刃。

（4）定勢時，劍身平行於身體右側，劍尖略向下，右臂微屈。

【意念】

意念在頭虛領，胯下沉，坐身，拔背伸指。抽劍要相對用力撐住，呼氣助勁。

（4）Point Forward in Empty Step

Continue to turn the upper body to the right and then to

圖3-53

the left. Bring the left foot a half step in and shift the weight onto the right foot to form a left Empty Step. At the same time, the right hand pulls the sword back to the right hip, with the blade at the right side of the body diagonally, and the tip pointing slightly down. The left Sword Fingers move backward and upward, passing under the chin, to point forward, at eyes level. Eyes look at the Sword Fingers (Figure 3-53).

Key Points

(1) The actions of the Sword Fingers pointing forward, the left toes touching the ground, and the upper body turning back to the left should cooperate with each other and finish at the same time.

(2) The Empty Step and the left Sword Fingers both point to 30° – 40° south of east.

(3) When pulling back the sword, move it in a downward arc with edge up; deliver the force to the edge.

(4) When the movement is completed, the blade of the sword is parallel to the right side of the body, the tip pointing slightly downward and the right arm bent slightly.

Keep in Mind

Maintaining the head up; sink the hip; move backward the body; draw the back up and extend the fingers. Draw back the sword with force. Exhale to increase the power.

十八、併步平刺（白猿獻果）

1. 墊步轉體

左腳略向左移，上體左轉。同時，左劍指內旋並向左畫弧至上體左前側，眼看前方（圖3-54）。

【要領】

左腳尖移於走勢正前，移步要輕緩。劍指水平向右畫弧，手心向左。

【意念】

鬆左胯移步，意注左側腰腎放鬆，左手向左畫弧，意想撥簾。

18. Thrust with Feet Together（White Ape Offers Fruit）

(1) Skip and Turn Body

Move the left foot to the left slightly. Turn the upper body

圖3-54

to the left. Meanwhile, rotate the left Sword Fingers inward and draw an arc towards the left front of the upper body. Eyes look ahead (Figure 3–54).

Key Points

Swing the left toes to point to the front. Move the foot lightly and slowly. The Sword Fingers draw an arc to the right horizontally, palm facing left.

Keep in Mind

Relax the left hip when stepping to the left. The left hand draws an arc to the left as if pushing aside a curtain.

2. 併步平刺

重心前移，右腳向左腳併步。同時，右手持劍外旋翻轉經腰間向前平刺，左劍指畫弧收至腰間，翻轉變掌，協調刺劍將掌托於右手下，手心向上，眼看前方（圖3–55）。

【要領】

（1）捧劍時左手也可為劍指，按個人習慣掌握。

（2）刺劍、併步、上體前移要協調一致。

（3）刺劍後，兩肩要鬆沉，兩臂微屈，兩肘向下。

【意念】

意注頭頂、胸含、背拔、腳踩、手伸，全身合勁，力貫劍尖而出。

(2) Thrust Sword and Feet Together

Shift the weight forward. Place the right foot beside the left foot. At the meantime, turn the right hand outward past the waist and thrust the sword forward with its blade flat. Move the left hand back to the waist in an arc and then change into an open palm to hold the back of the right hand, palm facing up. Eyes look ahead (Figure 3-55).

Key Points

(1) According one's habit, the left finger can maintain in the shape of a Sword Fingers to hold the sword with the right hand.

(2) The motions of thrusting sword, moving feet together and moving the upper body forward should cooperate with each

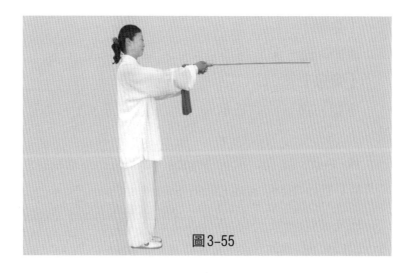

圖3-55

other.

(3) After thrusting the sword, relax the shoulders and bend the arms slightly with the elbows pointing down.

Keep in Mind

Draw the head up; tuck the chest in; draw the back up; push the ground with the foot and extend the arms. Collect the energy from the whole body and deliver the force to the tip of the sword.

十九、左弓步攔（迎風撣塵①）

1. 轉體繞劍

上體右轉，兩腿屈膝。同時，右手持劍內旋，使手心向外，隨轉體由前向上向後繞轉至頭右側稍後上方，左手變劍指隨右腕繞轉，眼看右後方（圖3–56）。

【要領】

轉體屈蹲，重心移於右腿，左腳跟再提起。

【意念】

意想右腰腎向右後畫圓，同時鬆右胯，配合以吸氣。

19. Parry in Left Bow Stance(Dusting in the Wind①)

(1) Turn Body and Swing Sword

Turn the upper body right and bend the knees. Meanwhile, turn the right hand inward until the palm facing out.

Following the body, move the sword upward then backward and stop at the upper right slightly behind the head. Turn the left hand into Sword Fingers and follow the right wrist. Eyes look at the upper back (Figure 3-56).

Key Points

Turn the body and bend knees to a half squat. Lift the left heel after shifting the weight onto the right leg.

Keep in Mind

Turn the right waist in an arc to the right back. Relax the right hip and inhale.

2. 上步繞劍

左腳向左前方上步，腳跟著地。右手持劍繼續向

圖3-56

後向下繞轉，左劍指外翻轉收於腹前，眼看右後方
（圖3-57）。

【要領】

（1）右手持劍向後繞轉時小臂要內旋，手心翻轉
向外，劍身斜立，劍柄領繞，劍貼身成立圓走向。

（2）上體右轉幅度要充分，眼隨轉體看右後方。

【意念】

此式氣沉、胯落、鬆肩、垂肘，氣直沉右腳底。

(2) Step Forward and Swing Sword

The left foot steps to the left front, with only the heel
touching the ground. The right hand continues to move the sword
backward and downward. The left Sword Fingers turn over and
draw back to the abdomen. Eyes look to the right back (Figure
3-57).

Key Points

（1）When swinging the sword backward, turn the right
forearm inward until the palm facing outward. Move the sword
in a vertical ellipse, the blade of the sword slanted and the
handle leading.

（2）The upper body makes a big turn to the right. Eyes
follow the body to look at the right back.

Keep in Mind

Sink the hips; relax the shoulders and sink the elbows.

Sink the energy（Qi）directly to the right foot.

3. 弓步攔劍

上體左轉，左腿屈膝前弓，右腿自然伸直，成左弓步。同時，右手持劍由右後方向左前上方攔架，力在劍刃，劍高與頭平，劍尖略低，並對準上體中線。攔架時臂要外旋，使手心斜向內，同時左劍指向左上繞舉於左額上方，眼看劍尖（圖3-58）。

【要領】

（1）攔劍時，劍要在上體右側隨身體右旋左轉，貼身繞一立圓。

（2）左弓步方向在東北方，為中心線偏北30°～

圖3-57

圖3-58

40°。

（3）攔劍高度同頭平，齊於左肩。

【意念】

（1）完成動作時兩腰腎鬆沉，襠走下弧，以腰帶動。

（2）攔劍時滿把握劍，腰手聯動，呼氣助勁。

(3) Parry in Bow Step

Turn the upper body to the left. Bend the left leg and extend the right leg naturally straight to form a left Bow Step. Meanwhile, the right hand moves the sword from the right back to the upper left front and parry at head level, the tip slightly lower, aligning with the centre of the upper body, force on the edge. As parrying, turn the arm outward, palm facing diagonally inward. At the same time, the left Sword Fingers move to the upper left of the forehead. Eyes look at the tip of the sword (Figure 3-58).

Key Points

（1）When parrying, along with the body turn to the right, turn the sword to the left, drawing a vertical ellipse close to the body.

（2）The left Bow Step points to the northeast, about 30° – 40° north of the centre of the body.

（3）When parrying, the right hand at head level, the tip of the sword at the left shoulder level.

Keep in Mind

（1）When the movement is completed, relax the waist. Led by the waist, move the crotch in a downward arc.

（2）Hold the sword in full grip. The waist and hand coordinate with each other. Exhale to increase power.

二十、右弓步攔（迎風撣塵②）

1. 擺腳繞劍

重心微向後移，左腳尖外擺，上體微左轉。同時，右手持劍上舉，向左後方回繞，眼看右手（圖3-59）。

圖3-59

20. Parry in Right Bow Stance（Dusting in the Wind②）

(1) Toes out and Swing Sword

Shift the weight backward slightly. Turn the upper body slightly to the left and swing the left toes outward. At the same time, raise the sword and move it to the left back. Eyes look at the right hand (Figure 3-59).

2. 收腳收劍

上體繼續左轉，右腳收至左腳內側，不可點地。同時，右手持劍在身體左側由上向後向下畫一立圓在左肋前，劍身貼近身體，左劍指落於右腕，眼隨劍向左後看（圖3-60）。

(2) Bring Foot in and Withdraw Sword

Continue to turn the upper body to the left. Bring the right foot beside the left foot without touching the ground. Meanwhile, the right hand holds the sword and draws a vertical ellipse backward at the left side of the body and in front of the left ribs, the blade close to the body. The left Sword Fingers are resting on the right wrist. Eyes follow the sword to look at the left back (Figure 3-60).

3. 弓步攔劍

上體右轉，右腳向右前方邁出，屈膝前弓，成右弓步。同時，右手持劍由下經體前向右前上方攔出，手心向外，高與頭平，劍尖略低，劍身斜向內，左劍指附於右腕部，眼看前方（圖3-61）。

要領及意念與「左弓步攔」動作相同，只是左右相反。

(3) Parry in Bow Step

Turn the upper body to the right. The right foot steps towards the right front and bend knee to form the right Bow Step. Meanwhile, past in front of the body, the right hand holds the sword to parry to the upper right front, palm facing out. The blade of the sword is placed obliquely inward at head level, the tip slightly lower. The left Sword Fingers still rest on the right wrist at this point. Eyes look ahead (3–61).

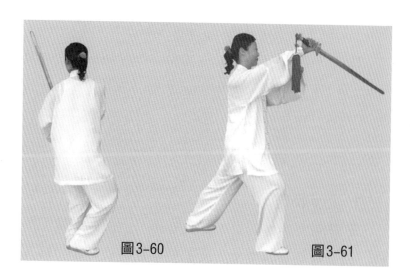

圖3-60　　　　圖3-61

The Key Points and Keep in Mind are the same as those for last form: "Parry in Left Bow Stance (Dusting in the Wind ①)", only in the opposite direction.

二十一、左弓步攔（迎風撣塵③）

身體重心微向後移，右腳尖外擺，其餘動作與「右弓步攔」各動作一致，唯方向相反。右手持劍攔出時，右臂外旋，手心斜向內，眼看劍尖。

要領與意念同前「左弓步攔」。

21. Parry in Left Bow Stance (Dusting in the Wind③)

Shift the weight slightly backward. Turn the right toes outward. The rest of the movement is same with that in last form, only in the opposite direction. As the right hand holds the sword to parry, turn the right arm outward, palm facing diagonally inward. Eyes look at the tip of the sword.

The Key Points and Keep in Mind are the same as those of "Parry in Left Bow Stance (Dusting in the Wind①)", only in the opposite direction.

二十二、進步反刺（順水推舟）

1. 上步收劍

右腳向前橫落蓋步，腳尖外撇，上體微右轉。同時，右手持劍屈腕下落，使劍柄落在胸前，劍尖轉向下，左劍指落於右腕部，眼看右方（圖3-62）。

【要領】

（1）蓋步後，身體重心落在兩腳。

（2）右手持劍屈腕下落時，前臂要外旋，上臂要向右肋靠，肘尖對準心窩，手心向外，拳眼向下，活把握劍，劍尖向下。

【意念】

意念上要鬆右胯，右腳輕靈蓋步，落劍時鬆右肩，下墜肘，平緩吸氣。

22. Step Forward and Plunge Backward

（Pushing the Boat with Current）

（1）Step Forward and Withdraw Sword

The right foot steps forward to form a Crossover Step, turn-

圖3-62

ing the toes outward. Turn the upper body slightly to the right. At the same time, move the sword down by bending the wrist to lay the hilt before the chest, the tip pointing downward. Place the left Sword Fingers on the right wrist. Eyes look to the right (Figure 3–62).

Key Points

(1) In the Crossover Step, the weight is shared by the feet.

(2) When bending the wrist to move down the sword, turn the forearm outward with the upper arm closing with the right ribs and the elbow pointing the heart. The right palm faces outward and the eye of the fist faces downward. Grip the sword loosely. The tip of the sword points down.

Keep in Mind

Relax the right hip. Make the Crossover Step lightly and gently. Relax the right shoulder; sink the elbow; inhale evenly as moving down the sword.

2. 轉體後刺

上體右轉不停，兩腿屈膝交叉半蹲成高坐盤，重心偏於右腳，左腳跟掀起。同時，右手經腹前向後立劍刺出，手心向體前一側；左劍指在腹前，對應刺劍向前（正東）指出，手心向下，兩臂平伸一線，眼看後方（圖3-63）。

【要領】

（1）半坐盤時，左膝抵住右膝膕窩，上體正直，不可彎腰低頭。

（2）後刺劍，兩手從腹前分展，右手向後直刺，左劍指向正東指出，劍與右臂成一直線，前指後刺同時完成。

【意念】

意注氣向右腳，轉腰、鬆胯、立身，呼氣助勁貫於劍尖。

(2) Turn Body and Thrust Backward

Continue to turn the upper body to the right. Bend the legs to a half squat to form a Crossover Step. With the left heel being off the ground the weight is mainly on the right leg. Mean-

圖3-63

while, move the right hand past the abdomen and stab the sword backward with its edge up, palm facing inward. The Sword Fingers move from the abdomen upward to the upper front (east), palm facing down. Two arms are extended on one straight line. Eyes look to the back (Figure 3–63).

Key Points

(1) In the Crossover Step, the left knee attaches the inside of the right knee. Keep the upper body upright, don't bend the waist or bow the head.

(2) When stabbing the sword backward, separate the hands apart in front of the abdomen. The right hand stabs toward the back; the left Sword Fingers point the front. The sword is on one line with the right arm. The stabbing backward and pointing forward are finished at the same time.

Keep in Mind

Focus the mind on: sink the energy to the right foot；turn the waist；relax the hip；draw the body up and exhale to deliver the force to the tip of the sword.

3. 弓步反刺

劍尖上挑，上體左轉，重心略起，左腳前進一步，成左弓步。同時，右臂屈肘，劍經頭側向前反手立劍刺出，手心向外，上臂貼近右耳旁，劍尖略低，左劍指收放於右腕部，眼看劍尖（圖3-64）。

【要領】

（1）反刺劍時，右臂、右肘、腕均應先屈後伸，隨腰轉由後向前探刺，力貫劍尖。

（2）上體略前傾，右臂貼近頭右側，右手與頭同高，臂與劍身在右手腕處成一小折角。

（3）此動是正弓步，探刺上體略有前傾。兩腳橫向距離為20公分左右。

【意念】

意注鬆腰鬆胯，轉腰送劍。上左腳時吸氣，探刺劍時呼氣。

(3) Thrust in Backhand with Bow Step

Tilt up the tip of the sword. Turn the upper body to the

圖3-64

left. Raise the weight up slightly. The left foot steps forward to form a left Bow Step. At the same time, bend the right elbow to move the sword from the right side of the head and stab it forward, the palm facing outward and the upper arm close to the right ear. The tip of the sword is a little lower than the blade. Draw the left Sword Fingers back to the right wrist. Eyes look at the tip of the sword (Figure 3-64).

Key Points

(1) When stabbing the sword in backhand, bend the right arm, the right elbow and the right wrist first and then extend them. Following the waist turning, thrust the sword forward with force to the tip.

(2) Lean the upper body slightly forward. The right arm is close to the right side of the head, hand at head level. The right wrist forms a small angle.

(3) Using the sword technique of Lean and Thrust (Tan Ci) in a forward Bow Step. The body slightly leans forward. The feet stand on parallel lines separately, which are apart about 20cm.

Keep in Mind

Pay attention to relax the waist and hips. Turn the waist to thrust the sword. Inhale while stepping forward and exhale while thrusting the sword.

二十三、反身回劈（*流星趕月*）

1. 轉體收劍

右腿屈膝，上體後倚，重心移至右腳。同時，劍收至臉前右側；而後上體右轉，左腳裏扣，左劍指仍附於右腕部，眼看劍尖（圖3-65）。

【要領】

右腿屈膝，重心後移時上體要後倚撐勁，左腳內扣130°。

【意念】

意注右胯根放鬆，肩鬆肘拉，以上體後倚帶劍，吸氣配合。

圖3-65

23. Turn Around to Chop (The Comet Chases the Moon)

(1) Turn Body and Withdraw Sword

Bend the right knee. Draw the upper body backward and shift the weight onto the right leg. Meanwhile, draw the sword back to the right front of the head. Then turn the upper body to the right and swing the left foot inward. The left Sword Fingers are still on the right wrist. Eyes look at the tip of the sword (Figure 3-65).

Key Points

As bending the right knee and shifting the weight backward, draw the upper body backward with the force and swing the left foot 130° inward.

Keep in Mind

Focus the mind on relaxing the base of the right hip and the shoulders. Push the elbow. Draw the upper body backward to lead the sword while inhaling.

2. 提腳舉劍

上體右轉不停，重心回移至左腿，右腳提起收至左踝骨內側。同時，右手持劍上舉，劍指落挎於左腹前，眼向左看（圖3-66）。

【要領】

（1）左腳移穩後再提右腳。

（2）右腳收至左踝骨處時，右腿要半屈蹲，上體直立。

【意念】

（1）動作連貫不斷勁，吸氣沉勁，氣向右腳沉，襠隨轉體走一個小圓弧。

（2）持劍右手與左腳上下對拉勁。

(2) Lift Foot and Raise Sword

Continue to turn the upper body to the right. Shift the weight onto the left leg. Lift the right foot and place it to the inside of the left ankle. Meanwhile, raise the sword and move the sword finger in left front of the abdomen. Eyes look to the left (Figure 3–66).

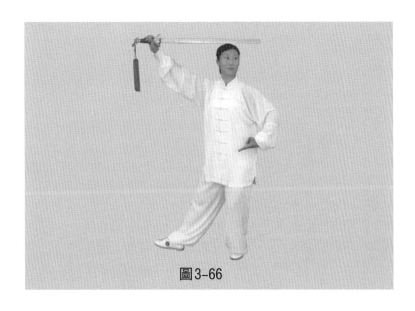

圖3-66

Key Points

（1）Lift the right foot after shifting the weight to the left foot.

（2）When bringing the right foot to the side of the left ankle, bend the right leg to a half squat and maintain the upper body upright.

Keep in Mind

（1）Keep the movement continuous without interrupted. Inhale and sink the energy （Qi） to the right foot. The crotch follows the body to move in a small arc.

（2）Push the right hand and the left leg in the opposite directions.

3. 弓步回劈

右腳向前偏右邁出，右腿屈膝前弓，重心前移成右弓步。同時，右手持劍隨轉體由上向右前劈出，左手劍指畫弧上繞至左額上方，手心斜向上，眼看劍尖（圖3-67）。

【要領】

（1）弓步回劈方向偏右30°，立劍平劈，臂與劍一線。上體正直，不可前傾。

（2）回劈劍、弓步和劍指上繞協調配合，同時完成，不可割裂。

【意念】

氣貫兩腳，勁達劍刃，右肩鬆沉。

(3) Chop Backward in Bow Step

The right foot steps to the right front. Bend the right knee and shift the weight forward to form a right Bow Step. At the same time, the right hand holds the sword, following the body, and chops down to the right front. The left Sword Fingers draw an arc to the upper left side of the forehead, palm facing diagonally up. Eyes look at the tip of the sword (Figure 3–67).

Key Point

(1) The direction of the bow step (also the chopping direction) is about 30° right to the front. Chop with the edge up and the arm aligning with the sword. Keep the upper body up-

圖3-67

right; don't bend forward.

（2）Chopping, stepping and raising the Sword Fingers should coordinate with each other and finish at the same time. Do not separate them.

Keep in Mind

Sink the energy（Qi）to the feet. Deliver the force to the edge of the sword. Relax and sink the right shoulder.

二十四、虛步點劍（燕子銜泥）

1. 落指收腳

劍指下落右腕部，左腳隨之收至右腳內側，不可點地，眼看劍尖（圖3-68）。

圖3-68

2. 轉體舉劍

上體左轉，左腳向起勢方向（正南）上步，腳跟著地，腳尖外撇。同時，右臂外旋，畫弧上舉，手心向上，劍尖向體後；左劍指經體前向身體左側上舉，手心向上，眼看前方（圖3-69）。

3. 虛步點劍

重心前移，左腳踏實，右腳上步在左腳前，腳尖點地成右虛步。同時，右手持劍向前下方點出，力注劍尖；點劍的同時，劍指下落於右腕部，眼看劍尖（圖3-70）。

【要領】

（1）本式動作要連貫、圓活，不可斷勁。

（2）點劍時，兩手相合，先下沉，再提腕前送

圖3-69　　　　　　　　圖3-70

下點，點劍與右腳虛步點地同時完成。上體保持中
正，不可前傾低頭。

【意念】

（1）全套動作胯部要鬆沉，步伐要輕靈，氣達
四肢。

（2）定勢時，全身勁聚丹田，呼氣助力，使勁
傳於劍身，貫於劍尖。

24. Point Sword in Empty Stance

(Swallow Picks up Mud with its Beak)

(1) Move Down Sword Fingers and Withdraw Foot

Move the Sword Fingers down to the right wrist. Withdraw
the left foot to the inside of the right foot without touching the
ground. Eyes look at the tip of the sword (Figure 3–68).

(2) Turn Body and Raise Sword

Turn the body to the left. The left foot steps forward (south),
only the heel touching the ground. Swing the toes outward.
Meanwhile, turn the right arm outward and raise the sword in
an arc, palm facing up and the tip of the sword pointing to the
back. Raise the left Sword Fingers, across in front of the body,
to the left side, palm facing up. Eyes look ahead (Figure
3–69).

(3) Point Sword in Empty Step

Shift the weight forward. Place the left foot on the ground

firmly. The right foot steps forward in front of the left foot, only the toes touching the ground to form a right Empty Step. Meanwhile, the right hand holds the sword and points it down to the lower front, delivering force to the tip. Move the Sword Fingers down to the right wrist. Eyes look at the tip of the sword (Figure 3-70).

Key Points

(1) The movement should be continuous and fluent. Deliver the force with no pause.

(2) When pointing down the sword, hold the hands together. Sink the wrist first and then lift it to point the sword down. The pointing is finished at the same time as the right foot touching the ground. Keep the upper body upright. Don't bend forward or bow the head.

Keep in Mind

(1) To complete the whole set of the movements need to relax the hips; step lightly and quickly. Deliver the energy (Qi) to the limbs.

(2) When the movement is completed, gather the energy of the entire body to Abdomen. Exhale to increase the power. Deliver the force through the blade of the sword to the tip.

二十五、獨立平托（挑簾式）

1. 插步繞劍

右腳向左腳左後方插步，腳前掌著地，兩腿屈膝半蹲。同時，右手外旋持劍在體前向上向左向下環繞，劍柄落於左腰前，手心向裏，劍身立劍平置於身體左側，左劍指隨右腕環繞，眼看劍尖（圖3-71）。

【要領】

繞劍插步時腰微左轉，帶動右腕外旋，協調一致，同步進行。上體正直，不可前俯。

【意念】

意注縮左胯，旋腰繞劍，氣向下沉。

圖3-71

Group 4

25. Level Sword and Stand on One Leg

(Lift Door Curtain)

(1) Swing Sword with Backward Crossover-Leg

Move the right foot to the left back of the left foot in a backward Crossover-Step, only the forefoot touching the ground; bend legs to half squats. Meanwhile, turn the right hand outward and move the sword upward, leftward and then downward in front of the body, laying the hilt of the sword in front of the left waist and the blade of the sword placed horizontally at the left side of the body with the edge up; the right palm faces inward. The left sword fingers follow the right wrist. Eyes look at the tip of the sword (Figure 3–71).

Key Points

When swinging the sword and stepping backward in a Crossover Step, turn the waist slightly to the left and lead the right wrist turned outward. The motions are co-ordinate with each other and progress at the same time. Keep the upper body upright. Do not bend forward.

Keep in Mind

Pull the left hip in and turn the waist to swing the sword. Sink the energy (Qi).

2. 提膝托劍

　　兩腳以前掌為軸，上體向右轉向正西，隨之左膝上提，右腿站立成右獨立步。同時，右手持劍隨轉體向上托架，立劍平置於頭右側上方，左劍指附於右臂內側，眼看前方（圖3-72）。

【要領】

　　（1）右手活把握劍，手心向外，劍身高於頭，力在劍刃向上架托，右手與右肩上下對應。

　　（2）提膝托劍同時完成，整體動作前後要連貫，不可割裂，要一氣呵成。

【意念】

　　注意屈胯含胸，頭上領，氣下沉，勁上達於劍身，吸氣，丹田與右手托劍對撐。

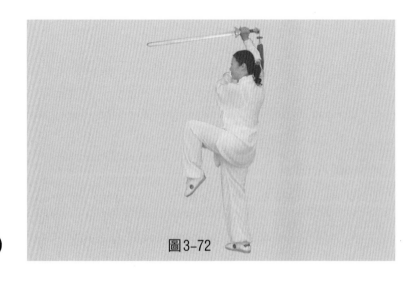

圖3-72

(2) Lift Knee and Raise Sword

Pivoting on both forefeet, turn the upper body to the west and lift the left knee to form a right One Leg Stance. Meanwhile, following the turning body, lift the sword up and place the blade horizontally at the upper right of the head with edge up. The left sword fingers are touching the inside of the right arm. Eyes look ahead (Figure 3-72).

Key Points

(1) The right hand hold the sword loosely, palm facing outward, the blade higher than the head, the force on the upper edge. The right hand and the right shoulder align vertically with each other.

(2) The motions of lifting the knee and raising the sword are finished at the same time. The entire movement should be continuous, without interruption.

Keep in Mind

Bend the hip and draw the chest in. Draw the head up and sink the energy (Qi). Deliver the force to the blade of the sword. Push the abdomen (Dantian) and the right hand in opposite directions. Inhale.

二十六、弓步掛劈（左車輪）

1. 轉體掛劍

左腳向前橫落，上體左轉，兩腿交叉成半坐盤式，右腳離地，重心主要移於左腳。同時，右手持劍向左後方穿掛，劍尖向後，左劍指附於右腕上，回頭眼看劍尖（圖3-73）。

【要領】

（1）掛劍時，隨上體轉動，右臂向下向後穿掛劍，劍身平行貼於身體左側，虎口向後，劍尖領先。

（2）掛劍轉體幅度要大，眼隨劍動，上體略前傾，但不可貓腰低頭。

【意念】

轉身掛劍慢呼氣，意在右肩向左胯合氣。

26. Wheeling Chop in Right Bow Step(Left wheeling)

(1) Turn Body and Stab Back

The left foot steps forward with the toes pointing to the left. Turn the body to the left, crossing the legs and squat. While lifting the right heel off the ground, shift the weight to the left leg. Meanwhile, stab the sword towards the left back with the tip pointing backward. The left sword fingers rest on the right wrist. Eyes look at the tip of the sword (Figure 3–73).

Key Points

(1) When stabbing back, the right arm follows the upper body and moves the sword downward and backward. The blade of the sword is close and parallel to the left side of the body. The "tiger mouth" faces back and the tip leads the sword.

(2) In this movement, the body makes a big turn. Eyes follow the sword. The upper body slightly leans forward, but do not stoop or bow the head.

Keep in Mind

When turning the body and stabbing back, exhale slowly. Deliver the energy (Qi) from the right shoulder to the left hip.

圖3-73

2. 弓步劈劍

上體右轉，右腳向前上步，右膝屈弓，重心主要移於右腿，左腿自然伸直，成右弓步。同時，右手持劍內旋翻腕，上舉向前劈下，立劍平劈，與肩同高；左劍指經後向上繞至頭左上方，手心向上，眼看前方（圖3-74）。

【要領】

弓步和劈劍方向均為正西，劍身與右臂平直一線，弓步時左腳跟不可掀起。

【意念】

呼氣助力，沉肩，沉胯。

(2) Chop in Bow Step

Turn the upper body to the right. The right foot takes a

圖3-74

step forward. Bend the right leg forward. Shift the weight onto the right leg and extend the left leg naturally to form a right Bow Step. At the same time, turn the right wrist inward and raise the sword to chop down with the edge up and the blade at shoulder level. Meanwhile, move the left sword fingers upward to the upper left of the head, palm facing up. Eyes look ahead (Figure 3-74).

Key Points

The directions of the Bow Step and the chopping are both to the west. The blade of the sword aligns with the right arm. The left heel should not be lifted off the ground in Bow Step.

Keep in Mind

Exhale to increase the power. Sink the shoulders and the hips.

二十七、虛步掄劈（右車輪）

1. 轉體掄劍

重心後移，上體右轉，右腳尖外撇，隨後右腳踏實，重心前移，右腿屈弓，左腳跟離地，兩腿交叉。同時，右手持劍在身體右側由下向後反手掄擺，左劍指畫弧落於右肩前，手心向下，劍指向後略向上，回頭眼看後方（圖3-75）。

【要領】

（1）上體向右轉體前略後坐，即重心前移轉體。

（2）向後掄擺劍時要先抽帶，活把握劍；後掄劍時要提腕貼身後掄，避免劍尖觸地。

（3）眼要隨劍轉，後掄擺劍回頭向後方看。

【意念】

意注右胯根鬆縮，氣向下沉，上體稍前傾，頭向前上頂。

27. Swing Chop in Right Empty Step（Right Wheeling）

（1）Turn Body and Swing Sword

Shift the weight backward. Turn the upper body to the right. Swing the right toes outward and place the entire foot on the ground solidly. Shift the weight forward. Bend the right leg forward and lift the left heel off the ground. Cross the legs. In the meantime, swing the sword backward at the right side of

圖3-75　　　　　　　　　　圖3-76

the body, palm facing out. The left sword fingers draw an arc in front of right shoulder, palm facing down and fingers pointing up and back. Eyes look to the back (Figure 3–75).

Key Points

(1) Before turning the upper body to the right, draw it backward slightly; shift the weight foreward (backward) first, then turn the body to the right.

(2) When swinging the sword backward, pull the sword first and grip it loosely, then raise the wrist and swing it backward close to the body. Avoid touching the ground with the tip.

(3) The eyes follow the sword and look to the back when the sword is swung backward.

Keep in Mind

Relax the base of the right hip. Sink the energy (Qi). Lean the upper body slightly forward. Draw the head up.

2. 上步舉劍

上體左轉，左腳向前上步，腳跟著地，腳尖外撇。同時，右手持劍外翻臂掄舉劍至頭右側上方，左劍指下落經腹前向左畫弧側舉在上體左側，眼看前方（圖3–76）。

【要領】

右臂掄舉劍時，臂要屈，不可伸直，劍柄高於頭，劍尖向後略低。

【意念】

勁沉於右腿，右腳為虛。吸氣，頭上領。

(2) Step Forward and Raise Sword

Turn the upper body to the left. The left foot takes a step forward, only the heel touching the ground and the toes turning outward. At the same time, the right hand turns outward and swings the sword to the upper right of the head. The left sword fingers draw an arc to the left across in front of the abdomen and stop at the left side of the upper body. Eyes look ahead (Figure 3-76).

Key Points

When swinging the sword, bend the right arm; do not be rigid. The hilt of the sword is above the head and the tip points backward, slightly lower than the blade.

Keep in Mind

Sink the energy (Qi) to the right leg; the foot is empty. Inhale and draw the head up.

3. 虛步劈劍

重心前移，右腳踏實，左腳向前上步，腳尖著地成右虛步。同時，右手持劍向前下掄劈，劍尖與膝同高，劍與右臂成一條斜線；左劍指向上畫圓，向前下落於右手腕處，眼看前下方（圖3-77）。

【要領】

（1）掄劈劍動作要連貫完成，不可停頓。臂要舒展繞圓順勢向前下劈，力點在劍下刃中下部。

（2）上右步、下劈劍及左劍指下落要協調一致，同時完成。

【意念】

落胯沉氣，呼氣助力，勁貫劍刃中下部。

(3) Chop in Empty Step

Shift the weight forward. Place the right leg solidly on the ground. The left foot takes a step forward with only the toes touching the ground, forming a right Bow Step. Meanwhile, swing and chop down with the sword; the tip stops at knee lev-

圖3-77

el, and the sword is aligned with the right arm. The left sword fingers move forward in an arc and rest on the right wrist. Eyes look to the lower front (Figure 3-77).

Key Points

(1) The swing and chop should be connected smoothly without pause. The arm should be stretched and moving in an arc to chop. The force is on the middle and back part of the lower edge of the sword.

(2) The step, the chop and the sword fingers are co-ordinated with each other and finished at the same time.

Keep in Mind

Sink the hips and the energy (Qi). Exhale to increase the power. The force is on the middle and back part of the edge of the sword.

二十八、撤步反擊（大鵬展翅）

1. 撤步合劍

重心放在左腿，右腳輕輕提起向右後方撤一步。同時，右手持劍，臂外旋，使劍尖由右向下向左畫一小圓，手心斜向上，左劍指停於右腕上方，眼看劍尖（圖3-78）。

28. Step Back to Strike Backward

(Phoenix Spreads Its Wings)

(1) Step Back and Roll Sword

Shift the weight onto the left leg. Lift the right foot gently and step towards the right back. Meanwhile, rotate the right arm outward and move the sword right, down, and left to draw an arc (rolling the sword), palm facing up diagonally. The left sword fingers rest above the right wrist. Eyes look at the tip of the sword (Figure 3–78).

2. 轉身擊劍

上體右轉，重心右移，右膝屈弓，左腿自然伸直，左腳跟外碾成右側弓步。同時，右手持劍隨上體

圖3-78

右轉向右後上方反擊劍，力在劍刃前端，劍尖斜向上，高與頭平；左劍指向左下方分開，高與胯平，手心向下，眼看劍尖（圖3-79）。

(2) Turn Body and Strike

Turn the upper body to the right. Shift the weight to the right. Bend the right knee forward, extend the left leg naturally straight, and turn the left heel outward to form a right Side Bow Step. In the meantime, the right hand follows the body and strikes with the sword to the upper right back, the force on the front part of the edge, the tip pointing up diagonally at head level. The left sword fingers move to the lower left at hip level, palm facing down. Eyes look at the tip of the sword (Figure 3-79).

圖3-79

【要領】

（1）撤步，擊劍方向為東北方向，定勢右弓步為側弓步（右腳尖方向在西北方向）。

（2）此勢為反擊劍（向右擊為反擊，向左擊為正擊），反擊劍時要在腰的帶動下，臂、肘、腕先屈後伸，使力達劍的前端。

（3）重心由左向右移動成右側弓步時，胯要下沉移動，襠走下弧，上體不可上竄。

【意念】

（1）合劍時，右肩要向左胯沉勁，肩胯相合，上體氣下沉。

（2）擊劍是在合身合勁的基礎上，轉身開胸，將合勁拉開，使劍擊出。呼氣助力，兩手注入一種對拉勁。

Key Points

（1）Take the step back to the northeast and strike with the sword in the same direction. When the movement is complete, the right Bow Step becomes a Side Bow Step with the toes pointing to the northwest.

（2）When striking back, the waist leads the arm, the elbow and the wrist to first bend and then extend to deliver the force to the forepart of the sword.

（3）When shifting the weight from the left to the right to

form a right Side Bow Step, sink the hip and move the crotch in a downward arc. Do not raise the upper body.

Keep in Mind

(1) When rolling the sword, sink the force from the right shoulder to the left hip to combine both. Sink the energy of the upper body.

(2) Based on the combination of the body and the force, turn the body and open the chest. Release the combined energy to strike with the sword. Exhale to increase the power. The hands forcefully push towards each other.

二十九、進步平刺（烏龍攪柱）

1. 提腳橫劍

上體左轉，重心左移，右腳裏扣。同時，右手持劍向左擺劍，劍身橫於體前，劍尖向右；左手劍指翻轉挎置左腰間，手心向上。

隨後上身再向右轉，提起左腳。同時，右手持劍翻掌向右後領帶，手心向下，將劍橫置於右胸前，劍尖向前；左劍指向上繞再落於右肩前，手心向下，眼看右前方（圖3-80）。

【要領】

（1）以腰帶臂，以臂領劍，劍走平弧。

（2）轉腰提左腳、橫劍與劍指繞轉要同時到位。

【意念】

腰部帶脈先左後右走一個回環圈，腰帶臂領劍走平擺，配合吸氣，一氣呵成。

29. Step Forward to Thrust

（Black Dragon Coils Around Pole）

(1) Lift Foot and Level Sword

Turn the upper body and shift the weight to the foot. Turn the right toes inward. Meanwhile, move the sword to the left and stop with the blade across in front of the body, the tip pointing to the right. The left sword fingers turn over and move back to the left waist, palm facing up.

Then turn the upper body to the right. Lift the left foot.

圖3-80

Meanwhile, the right hand turns over and draws the sword to the right back, palm facing down; place the sword horizontally in front of the right chest, the tip pointing forward. The left sword fingers move up first then stop in front of the right shoulder, palm facing down. Eyes look to the right front (Figure 3-80).

Key Points

(1) The waist leads the arm and the arm leads the sword. Move the sword in a horizontal arc.

(2) Turning waist and lifting the left foot, drawing the sword across and moving the sword fingers around all should be finished at the same time.

Keep in Mind

Move the "Dai Mai" to the left first then to the right. (Dai Mai is located around the waist like a belt; there are a few acupuncture points on it) The waist also leads the arm to swing the sword horizontally. Co-ordinated by inhaling, the movement is completed as a coherent whole.

2. 弓步平刺

上體左轉，左腳向前落步，腳尖外撇，而後重心前移；右腳上步屈膝前弓，左腿自然伸直，成右弓步。同時，右手持劍向下捲裏，經右腰側向前刺出，高與胸齊，手心向上；左劍指隨之翻轉經腹前向左向上繞至左側頭上方，眼看劍尖（圖3-81）。

【要領】

（1）劍捲落時要隨上體沉降。右臂外旋，右手心翻轉向上。劍尖不要外擺。劍尖指向正西。

（2）左腳落步及右腳上步要連貫。上步不要「砸夯」，步伐輕靈，褶走下弧。

（3）刺劍要轉腰順肩，上體正直，不要前俯，臂與劍成一直線。

（4）刺劍、弓腿、劍指上舉要同時完成。

【意念】

（1）肩、胯部要放鬆，身體下沉要平穩，重心移動走下弧。

（2）呼氣助力，勁貫劍尖，眼要隨劍走勢轉視。

圖3-81

(2) Thrust with the Sword Flat in Bow Step

Turn the upper body to the left. The left foot steps forward, the toes turning outward. Shift the weight forward. The right foot steps forward. Bend the leg and stretch the left leg naturally to form a right Bow Step. Meanwhile, revolve the sword downward and, from the right side of the waist, thrust the sword out at chest level, palm facing up. The left sword fingers turn over, following the movement. They fall down to the abdomen first and then move leftward and upward to the upper left of the head. Eyes look at the tip of the sword (Figure 3-81).

Key Points

(1) When revolving downward, the sword should follow the upper body to move down. Turn the right arm outward to make the right palm facing up. Point the tip of the sword to the west; do not swing it outward.

(2) Placing the left foot and the right foot stepping should be connected smoothly without a pause. Step lightly. The crotch moves in a downward arc.

(3) While thrusting the sword, turn the waist and push the shoulder to the same direction of the sword. The upper body is upright. Do not bend forward. The arm should be aligned with the sword.

(4) Thrusting the sword, bending the leg and raising the

sword fingers should all be finished at the same time.

Keep in Mind

（1）Relax the shoulder and hip. Lower the body stably. The weight moves in a downward arc.

（2）Exhale to increase the power and deliver the force to the tip of the sword. The eyes follow the sword.

三十、丁步回抽（懷中抱月）

重心後移，右腳撤至左腳內側，腳尖點地成右丁步。同時，右手持劍屈肘回抽，置於左腹旁，手心向裏，劍身側立，劍尖斜向上，左劍指附於劍柄，眼看劍尖（圖3-82）。

【要領】

（1）抽劍時，右手外旋，將劍向上托，隨後再向後向下弧形抽回。

（2）右腳收回點地，與左腳距離在一腳之內，超過一腳距離就成虛步。

【意念】

放鬆右胯，吸氣向左腳下沉。

30. Withdraw Sword in T- Step（Holding the Moon）

Shift the weight backward. Place the right foot beside the left foot, the toes touching the ground to form a right T-shape

Step. At the same time, bend the right elbow to withdraw the sword and place it to the left side of the abdomen, palm facing inward. The blade is erected and the tip points up diagonally. The left sword fingers rest on the hilt. Eyes look at the tip (Figure 3–82).

Key Points

(1) When withdrawing the sword, turn the right hand outward and lift the sword up, then move it to the lower back in an arc to the left abdomen.

(2) For the T–Step, the right toes are less than 20cm apart from the left foot. Otherwise, it would form an Empty Step.

Keep in Mind

Relax the right hip. Inhale and sink energy to the left

圖3-82　　　　　　　　　　　　　　　圖3-83

foot.

三十一、旋轉平抹（風掃梅花）

1. 擺步橫劍

右腳向前落步，腳尖外擺，上體稍右轉。同時，右手持劍翻掌向下，劍身橫於胸前，左劍指附於右腕，眼看劍尖（圖3-83）。

【要領】

（1）上體右轉90°，劍尖橫置時，兩臂在胸前半屈成圓弧。

（2）轉體、擺右腳、橫置劍要協調一致，同時完成。

【意念】

意注右腳，氣向下沉。轉身帶步、帶劍，勁走弧線，兩手與背對撐。

31. Turn Body and Slide Sword

(Wind Sweeps the Plum Blossoms)

(1) Toes Out and Sword across the Body

The right foot steps forward with the toes outward. Turn the upper body slightly to the right. At the same time, turn over the right hand to make the palm facing down; placc the blade of the sword across in front of the chest. The left sword fingers stay on the right wrist. Eyes look at the tip of the sword

(Figure 3–83).

Key Points

(1) Turn the upper body 90° to the right. When placing the sword across, the arms are arched in front of the chest.

(2) Turning the body, swinging the foot and placing the sword across should be done in coordination with each other and finish at the same time.

Keep in Mind

Focus the mind on the right foot. Sink the energy (Qi). Turn the body to lead the step and the sword. Deliver the force in an arc. Push the hands and the back in opposite directions.

2. 扣步抹劍

上體右轉不停，左腳在右腳前扣步，兩腳尖相對成內八字。同時，右手持劍隨轉體由左向右平抹，力在劍刃，左手劍指在右腕處不動，眼看劍身（圖3-84）。

【要領】

（1）身體轉至背向起勢方向，即面向北。

（2）抹劍高度與胸平，兩臂撐圓，以腰轉帶劍向右平抹，力點在劍刃上滑動。

（3）下肢微屈，不可站直。

【意念】

眼隨身轉。以身體為軸，以手領劍，勁沿劍刃繞圓。呼氣助力，轉動平穩勻緩。

(2) Slide Sword with Toes in

The upper body turns to the right. The left foot steps in front of the right foot. Both feet form a "/ \" shape. Meanwhile, the right hand follows the body and slides the sword from the left to the right, the force on the edge. The left sword fingers stay on the right wrist. Eyes look at the blade of the sword (Figure 3-84).

Key Points

(1) Turn the body to the direction that one backs at the Commencing, the north.

(2) The sliding sword is at chest level. The arms are arched. Use the waist to lead the sword sliding to the right. The

圖3-84

force is moving along the edge.

(3) Bend the legs slightly. Do not stand straight.

Keep in Mind

The eyes follow the body. Use the body as the axle and lead the sword by the hand. The force runs along the edge. Exhale to increase the power. Move evenly and stably.

3. 虛步分劍

　　以左腳掌為軸繼續向右後轉身，右腳隨轉體後撤一步，而後重心移至右腳，左腳尖點地成左虛步。兩手撐勁抹劍不停，在成虛步時，兩手左右分開，落於兩胯外側，手心均向下，劍身斜置於身體右側，劍尖裏擺向前，身體轉向起勢方向，眼看前方（圖3-85）。

圖3-85

【要領】

（1）整勢身體向右旋轉一周，轉身，抹劍要平穩連貫，速度均勻，上體正直，不可左右搖晃或前俯後仰。

（2）扣步、擺步要緊湊，保持上體原地轉動，兩腿要屈曲，不可直立。

（3）擺步腳跟先著地，扣步、撤步腳掌先著地，而後全腳著地，動作要輕靈。

【意念】

身體放鬆下沉，頭向上領勁，以呼氣完成動作。

（3）Separate Sword in Empty Step

Pivoting on the left forefoot, turn the body to the right. The right foot follows the body and takes a step backward. Then shift the weight backward onto the right foot, and the left toes touches the ground to form a left Empty Step. Meanwhile, the two hands keep arched and slide the sword continuously and forcefully. Separate the hands apart and move them respectively down to the sides of the hip, palms facing down. The blade of the sword is placed slantingly at the right side of the body, the tip pointing inward. The body faces the same direction as the Commencing (Figure 3–85).

Key Points

（1）In this movement, the body turns a whole circle to the

right. Turn the body and slide the sword steadily, continuously and evenly. Keep the upper body upright. Do not swing to the left or right. Do not bend forward or backward.

（2）The Toes in Step connects to the swinging heel closely. Keep the upper body turn at the original place. Bend the legs. Do not stand straight.

（3）When the right foot steps forward, the right heel touches the ground first. In Toes in Step and Withdraw Step, the forefoot touches the ground first, then the entire foot. The act should be light and gentle.

Keep in Mind

Relax and sink the entire body. Draw the head up. Exhale to complete the movement.

三十二、弓步直刺（指南針）

上體微下沉，左腳提起向前邁步，重心前移，左腿屈膝前弓，右腿自然伸直，成左弓步。同時，兩手收至腰間，右手立劍向前刺出，左劍指一同向前伸出附於右腕部，眼看前方（圖3-86）。

【要領】

（1）左腳邁步時，要先輕輕提起收至右腳內側再向前邁。

（2）持劍右手與劍指走後弧共同收至腰兩側，

同時向前刺出，要與身體中線對準，高與胸平。

【意念】

氣向下沉，邁步吸氣。刺劍呼氣助力，力達劍尖。

32. Thrust forward in Bow Step（Compass）

Lower the upper body slightly. Lift the left foot and take a step forward. Shift the weight forward. Bend the left knee and extend the right leg naturally straight to form a left Bow Step. At the same time, the hands move back to the sides of the waist. The right hand thrusts the sword forward. The left sword fingers move forward and stay on the right wrist. Eyes look ahead (Figure 3–86).

Key Points

（1）When the left foot stepping forward, lift it gently first

圖3-86

and bring it in beside the right foot, and then step forward.

（2）Both hands move back to the sides of the hip in an arc, and then move forward at the same time. The sword points to the opponent's centre of the body at chest level.

Keep in Mind

Sink the energy（Qi）. Inhale when stepping forward. Exhale to increase the power to thrust the sword, the force going to the tip.

收 式（抱劍歸原）

1. 後坐接劍

重心後移，右腿屈膝後坐，上體右轉。同時，右手持劍屈臂收手，將劍後引至右胸側，手心向裏，左劍指隨右手屈臂回收，肘尖向前，劍指變掌附於劍柄，眼看劍柄（圖3-87）。

【要領】

接劍時，左掌心向外，拇指向下，掌心貼住護手，兩肘與肩同高，兩肩要鬆，不要聳肩。

【意念】

右胯鬆，背後倚，上體正直，坐身吸氣。

Closing（Return the Sword to Its Original Position）

（1）Sit Back and Take Over Sword

Shift the weight backward. Bend the right leg and sit back.

Turn the upper body to the right. Meanwhile, bend the right elbow to bring the sword backward to the right side of the chest, palm facing inward. Bend the left elbow forward and bring back the sword finger. Turn the sword fingers into an open palm and rest it on the hilt. Eyes look at the hilt (Figure 3-87).

Key Points

When taking over the sword, the left palm faces outward, the thumb pointing down, and the centre of the palm contacting closely to the hilt. The elbows are at shoulder level. Relax the shoulders; do not lift them.

Keep in Mind

Relax the right hip and draw the back backward. Keep the upper body upright. Inhale while sitting back.

圖3-87

2. 上步收式

上體左轉，重心前移於左腿，右腳向前跟步，與左腳平行開立，與肩同寬。同時，左手接劍上舉，經體前下落收於身體左側，右手變為劍指，向下向後上舉，再向前下落於身體右側，眼看前方（圖3-88）。

【要領】

（1）換握劍後，左手持劍向上向前向下畫弧，與右手劍指向下向後向上畫弧要對稱相應，並與重心前移協調配合。

（2）右腳跟進及兩腿慢慢站立，要與右劍指協調一致。

【意念】

（1）左胯放鬆，屈膝上步、兩臂環繞時要吸氣。

圖3-88

（2）右劍指下落，兩腿站立，上體上升要平緩呼氣，眼平視前方。

（2）Step Forward to Close the Form

Turn the upper body to the left and shift the weight onto the left leg. The right foot steps forward to be parallel to the left foot. The feet apart are the same as the shoulder's width. At the same time, the left hand takes over the sword and moves across the front of the body and down to the left side of the body. The right hand turns into a sword fingers, moves downward, then to the upper back and then forward and downward to the right side of the body. Eyes look ahead (Figure 3–88).

Key Points

（1）After handing over the sword, the left hand holding the sword draws an arc upward and forward and downward, corresponding with the movement of right sword fingers moving downward, backward and upward, which is coordinated with shifting the weight forward.

（2）The right foot stepping forward and the legs standing straight slowly are coordinated in time with the sword fingers.

Keep in Mind

（1）Relax the left hip. Inhale while bending the knee to step forward and the arms moving.

（2）The legs stand up while the right sword fingers fall

down. Exhale slowly while raising the upper body. Eyes look to the front.

3. 併步還原

左腳向右腳併攏，還原成預備式（圖3-89）。

【要領】

同預備式，稍靜片刻。

【意念】

思想恢復無極狀態，全身內外放鬆，眼神內收，意存丹田，深吸氣數次。

(3) Feet Together to Original Position

Move the left foot close to the right foot, and resume the stance for preparation at the beginning (Figure 3–89).

圖3-89

Key Points

The Key Points are same as those in the Preparation. Keep calm for a moment.

Keep in Mind

Resume the mind into the state of Wu Ji (The state of mind in peace, calm and empty). Relax the entire body inside and outside. Bring the sight in. Focus the mind on Dantian. Breathe deeply several times.

附　32式太極劍動作佈局路線圖

　　熟悉並掌握套路動作線路佈局變化十分重要，因為步法的變化，落腳之位置和方向，不僅影響套路演練的連貫性和美感，更重要的是它確保了每個招式的方向、位置和根基的穩固。

　　套路的練習目的不僅在於熟練動作，還包含了對肢體動作乃至招式之間的起承轉合的體悟，對於在攻防實踐中的運用招式有直接的影響，在增強表演觀賞效果方面也有重要的作用（見附圖）。

Appendix Path Map of the 32-form Tai Chi Sword Movements

It is important to understand the path of the TaiJi forms. The location, the direction, and the translation between the steps have a great impact on the coherence of the whole form. More important, the path provides a solid foundation for each movement. When practising, one should not only be familiar with the movements, but also understand the connection between the movements, which is more important when applying to attacking and defending (see the figure on Page 218).

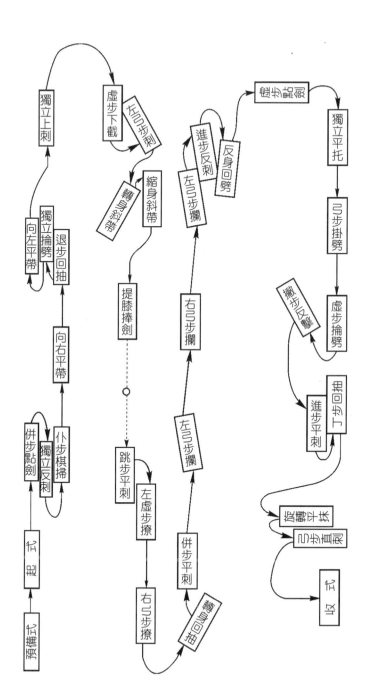

獨立上刺

虛步下截

左弓步刺

向左平帶

獨立掄劈

退步回抽

縮身斜帶

轉身斜帶

獨立平托

弓步掛劈

虛步掄劈

撤步反擊

進步反刺

反身回劈

左弓步攔

進步平刺

丁步回抽

右弓步攔

向右平帶

提膝捧劍

右弓步攔

左弓步攔

併步點劍

仆步橫掃

獨立反刺

跳步平刺

左虛步撩

併步平刺

轉身回抽

弓步直刺

抹轉身斜

收式

起式

右弓步撩

預備式

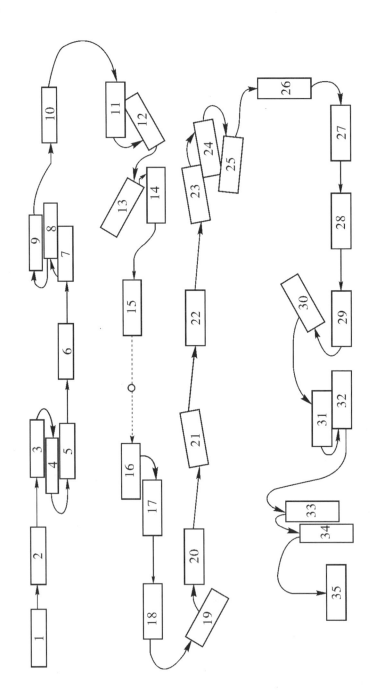

1. Preparation

2. Commencing

3. Point Sword with Feet Together

4. Stand on One Leg and Thrust

5. Sweep Sword in Crouch Step

6. Withdraw Sword to the Right

7. Withdraw Sword to the Left

8. Swing and Chop with One Leg Standing

9. Step Back and Withdraw Sword

10. Thrust Upward with One Leg Standing

11. Intercept Downward with Empty Step

12. Thrust in Left Bow Step

13. Turn Body and Withdraw Sword Diagonally

14. Retreat and Withdraw Sword

15. Lift Knee and Hold Sword with Both Hands

16. Hop and Thrust Sword with Blade Flat

17. Slice Sword Upward with Left Empty Stance

18. Slice Sword Upward with Right Bow Step

19. Turn Around and Withdraw Sword

20. Thrust with Feet Together

21. Parry in Left Bow Stance

22. Parry in Right Bow Stance

23. Parry in Left Bow Stance

附 32式太極劍動作佈局路線圖

32式太極劍

學與練

彩色圖解太極武術

定價220元

定價220元

定價220元

定價220元

定價350元

定價350元

定價350元

定價350元

定價350元

定價350元

定價350元

定價350元

定價350元

定價220元

定價220元

定價220元

定價350元

定價220元

定價350元

定價350元

定價220元

定價220元

定價220元

太極武術教學光碟

太極功夫扇
五十二式太極扇
演示：李德印 等
(2VCD)中國

夕陽美太極功夫扇
五十六式太極扇
演示：李德印 等
(2VCD)中國

陳氏太極拳及其技擊法
演示：馬虹(10VCD)中國
陳氏太極拳勁道釋秘
拆拳講勁
演示：馬虹(8DVD)中國
推手技巧及功力訓練
演示：馬虹(4VCD)中國

陳氏太極拳新架一路
演示：陳正雷(1DVD)中國
陳氏太極拳新架二路
演示：陳正雷(1DVD)中國
陳氏太極拳老架一路
演示：陳正雷(1DVD)中國
陳氏太極拳老架二路
演示：陳正雷(1DVD)中國
陳氏太極推手
演示：陳正雷(1DVD)中國
陳氏太極單刀・雙刀
演示：陳正雷(1DVD)中國

郭林新氣功
(8DVD)中國

本公司還有其他武術光碟
歡迎來電詢問或至網站查詢
電話：02-28236031
網址：www.dah-jaan.com.tw

原版教學光碟